QUAKER CLASSICS

IN BRIEF

WM. PENN'S NO CROSS NO CROWN
Anna Cox Brinton

BARCLAY IN BRIEF
Eleanore Price Mather

THE INWARD JOURNEY
OF ISAAC PENINGTON
Robert J. Leach

PENDLE HILL PUBLICATIONS

QUAKER CLASSICS IN BRIEF

Published as a PENDLE HILL PAPERBACK
First Printing June 1978

For information address Pendle Hill,
Wallingford, Pennsylvania

QUAKER CLASSICS IN BRIEF is composed of three pamphlets
originally published as Pendle Hill Historical Studies:

> #3 *Barclay in Brief* (1942)
> #6 *The Inward Journey of Isaac Penington* (1944)
> #7 *William Penn's* NO CROSS, NO CROWN (1944)

Later these works were assigned numbers 28, 29, and 30 in the
regular Pendle Hill pamphlet series. In previous editions each
appeared with an individual foreword by Howard H. Brinton
(1884-1973). In the present collection these have been condensed
into one.

Library of Congress catalog card number 78-57741
ISBN 0-87574-904-6
June 1978: 2,000

Printed in the United States of America
by Sowers Printing Company, Lebanon, Pennsylvania

FOREWORD

by

HOWARD H. BRINTON

THE publication of the works of William Penn, Robert
Barclay, and Isaac Penington make available in condensed
form the thought of three early leaders of the Society of
Friends whose writings are too lengthy for the present
mood. As Penn himself puts it, large books "especially in
these days grow burdensome both to the pockets and
minds of too many."

Penn deals with practice, Barclay with belief, and
Penington with inward experience. *No Cross No Crown*
began as a tract for the times of the extravagant Stuart
kings and ended as Penn's religious legacy to his country
and to the world of Christians. The glory of Christianity
being, as Penn insists, the purity of those who profess it, the
cure for Chistendom's defection can only come through
daily self-denial and through worship, by which is meant
"waiting patiently, yet watchfully and intently upon God."

Pride, power, worldly honor and respect, rank, wealth,
luxury, and every form of excess are adverse both to
religion and to the public welfare. The temperance Penn
pleads for is both politically and religiously good. "True
Godliness," he writes in the most famous sentence in *No
Cross No Crown,"* does not take men out of the world, but
enables them to live better in it and excites their endeavours
to mend it."

Barclay's achievement lies in his extraordinary synthesis
of the mystical or inward, that is, the experienced side of

iii

religion, and the evangelical or outward, that is, the historical side. The atonement he treats both as an historical fact and also as an inward process eternally renewed. Equally noteworthy is the balance which he maintains in distinguishing between the human and the divine, and herein lies his principal message for the present day. Calvinism, against which his book is mainly directed, created so profound and unbridgeable a chasm between man and God that man could never in this life time hope to be freed from the ruinous effects of inherited sin. Though Barclay shared much of Calvin's pessimism regarding the "natural man," yet he perceived that there is a seed of the divine in him which, if not resisted, will grow and transform him into its own likeness, making man one with God.

As for Penington, his life and writings reveal the purest, finest, and most genuine mysticism which has appeared in the Society of Friends. He was the first convert to the movement to write with literary taste and scholarly knowledge. Though not so practical as Penn, and less systematic than Barclay, he is surpassed by none in his excellent, fervent, vivid sense of the Divine Presence within. All else seemed to him an unsubstantial "world of shadows" which served only to obscure the brilliance of the Inward Light. The prevailing faith of our age is the reverse of that of Penington, for men's attention is now so generally centered in the outward world of the senses that the world within seems only shadow. The sickness of our time is due to the lack of balance resulting from a failure to nurture the inward spiritual life without which life as a whole has no meaning.

William Penn's

NO CROSS NO CROWN

Abridged by
ANNA COX BRINTON

.

PENDLE HILL PAMPHLET 30

INTRODUCTION

THE title of William Penn's most widely known religious book, *No Cross No Crown,* was bequeathed him
by Thomas Loe. It was through the ministry of this traveling Friend from Oxford that the principles of Quakerism
were first made known to him. As a boy of twelve he had
heard Loe preach, on Admiral Penn's invitation, in their
Irish home in County Cork. Young William was so struck
by the impression which this sermon made upon the entire
household that he wondered if they might not all turn
Quaker. At twenty-three, when in Ireland on his father's
business, Penn again heard Thomas Loe who spoke on the
words "There is a faith that overcomes the world and there
is a faith that is overcome by the world." Penn's convincement was by this time well under way. The fashionable
side of London life no longer interested him. The diarist
Pepys was told that William had become "a Quaker again
or some very melancholy thing." A year later William Penn
was called to the death bed of Thomas Loe. "Taking me
by the hand," writes Penn, "he spake thus, 'Dear heart, bear
thy cross, stand faithful for God and bear thy testimony in
thy day and generation, and God will give thee an eternal
crown of glory, that none shall ever take from thee. There is
not another way. This is the way the holy men of old
walked in and it shall prosper.' "

Soon after Loe's death Penn was confined for eight months
in the Tower of London on a charge of blasphemy. One
outcome of this leisure was his earliest version of *No Cross
No Crown,* a one-hundred-and-eleven-page pamphlet printed
in 1669. The argument was practical, a young man's plea

to eight of his personal friends, whom he identifies by their initials in the preface, to leave off pride, indulgence, foppishness and extravagance that debauches the rich and grinds down the poor. The marks of social distinction must go too, "hat-honor, titular respects," fashionable clothes and recreations. "Be you entreated," says Penn, "to eye that Divine principle engrafted on your minds, in all its holy, meek and self-denying instructions, that being mostly exercised thereby, you may be weaned from the glittering follies of the world and sensibly experiment the delights of the soul which are the inseparable companions of such retirements." The Cambridge Platonist, Henry More, wrote Penn regarding this pamphlet that he thought it "in the main very sober and good, though it may be over strict in some things."

To modern taste the phrase *No Cross No Crown* smacks too strongly of what Penn calls the "recompense of reward." We prefer to think that righteousness is sought solely for its own sake. But it must be admitted that both thought and words are Scriptural, and to the early Friends the propriety of such language was unquestioned. Both Testaments abound in promises of reward. The author of the Epistle to the Hebrews pressed on "toward the mark for the prize," the athlete's prize which was the crown or wreath of wild olive, and Paul wrote of Jesus that "for the joy that was set before him" he endured the cross.

The crown which results from the cross is the invisible sign of "temperance and sanctity of the mind." Penn's negative form of the antithesis helps toward our tolerance of his title. In his conclusion Penn, with his sturdy realism and his strong sense of rhythm, boldly carries further the contrast: "No cross, no crown; no temperance, no happiness; no virtue, no reward; no mortification, no glorification."

vii

"Mind not," he continues, "the difficulties of your march. Great and good things were never enterprised and accomplished without difficulty, which does but render their enjoyment more pleasant and glorious in the end."

The best in Penn's later social program is already present in this first edition of *No Cross No Crown*. From prison he could impartially assess the inequalities of privilege and resources in England. Already he knew that good men make a good nation. He pleads for integrity and personal responsibility. Honor all men, shun pride, behave seriously, be content with little: so shall there be enough for all, rents reduced, intelligent husbandry, happy homes, human beings serving as "stewards to each other's exigencies." "When the pale faces are more commiserated, the griped bellies relieved, the naked backs clothed; when the famished poor, the distressed orphan, God's works and your fellow creatures, are provided for, then I say, if then, it will be early enough for you to plead the indifferency of your pleasures."

But Penn was not ascetic. He valued outward as well as inward well-being. He would have goods equitably distributed and a plenty for all, but men's minds should not be set on money. To uphold this, as all his other arguments, he is ready with a scriptural anecdote. "If he that had loved God and his neighbor and kept the commandments from his youth" was excluded from being a disciple because he sold not all and followed Jesus, it was because Christ knew "for all his brags, that his mind was rivetted therein," the implication being that if this rich young man had enjoyed his possessions with "Christian indifference" they might have been continued.

Half or more than half of this pamphlet is quotation. "This is the way the holy men of old walked in," Thomas Loe had said, "and it shall prosper." From these men of old and from women too, so far as he could quote them, Penn supplies his readers with actual statements, having observed "the power which examples and authorities have put upon the minds of the people, above the most reasonable and pressing arguments." Biblical characters take the lead throughout, though in Part II pious pagans precede the early Christians who are followed by men and women of more modern times.

In the years which followed his first imprisonment, William Penn was engaged in a steady struggle for liberty of conscience. "Force," he says, "may make a hypocrite, 'tis faith grounded upon knowledge and consent that makes a Christian." "The Christian religion entreats all but compels none." Persecution was raging all through this time and informers, who were called by George Fox "the devil's nuthooks," were constantly besetting Friends, breaking up their meetings, depriving them of their goods, and throwing them into jail. Penn often shared these trials.

In 1670, Admiral Penn died. His son William was now twenty-six, handsome, wealthy, and in good standing with the king. At twenty-eight he married Gulielma Springett and with her lived a happy, active life, traveling in the ministry, arguing with opponents, publishing pamphlets. He accompanied George Fox and a few others on a visit to Holland and Germany.

In this period Penn's idea of a settlement in the New World took definite shape. He participated in the development of New Jersey and in 1681 received from Charles II a huge grant of land in payment of debts to his father. This tract the king called Pennsylvania.

While William Penn was projecting his "Holy Experiment," preparing its Frame of Government, and collecting colonists, *No Cross No Crown* was still brewing in his mind.

He had not yet fully acquitted himself of his debt to Thomas Loe.

In 1675, the Second Day's Morning Meeting which had charge of Quaker publications directed that *No Cross No Crown* be reprinted, but five years later it was still in process of emendation and the second edition did not finally appear until 1682, the year of Penn's first voyage to America. This second edition of six hundred pages in small octavo became far more widely known than the early pamphlet. It was reprinted more than fifty times and was a standby in meeting house and family libraries.

At least five translations of *No Cross No Crown* have been published. William Sewell brought out a Dutch version in Amsterdam in 1687. There are two French translations, the first published in Bristol, 1746, is by Claude Gay. The second, printed in London, 1793, is by Edward P. Beidel. There were also two German translations, a Pyrmont imprint of 1825 by George Uslar, and a London edition, 1847, from the press of J. Wertheimer.

Norman Penney's London edition, 1930 (466 pages), is the most convenient modern reprint. William Charles Braithwaite in the *Second Period of Quakerism,* draws a detailed comparison between the 1682 edition and the pamphlet of 1669. The pamphlet was never reprinted but a number of copies are extant.

The present abbreviation has taken account of both versions, and in three passages—retreats, p. 13, the tempter and the preserver, p. 21, and sitting loose to possessions, p. 32,— the amplification of 1694 is included. In reducing the text to one-half the compass of the early version and one-tenth the size of the 1682 edition, the whole argument has been preserved. The quotations are mainly omitted. It is noteworthy that the sections on society and the public good belong to the Tower of London version; those on faith and worship to the 1682 edition. Enough of Penn's religious phraseology is included to show that he accepted the terms of his time. The world, the flesh, the devil, hell, and the anguish of the damned are mentioned, though not dwelt upon.

The whole emphasis is on conduct as the expression of obedience to God. Every encouragement is given for man to mend his ways. Says William Penn to his reader: "Thou hast to do, I grant thee, with great patience, but that also must have an end: therefore provoke not that God that made thee to reject thee."

More characteristic is such an exhortation as this: "O Reader, What rests to us, then, that we must do, to be thus witnesses of his power and love? Come Reader be like him, for this transcendent joy lift up thy head above the world, then thy salvation will draw nigh indeed."

A hundred years after the appearance of the second edition, Charles Lamb wrote to Samuel Taylor Coleridge, "I am just beginning to read a most capital book, good thoughts in good language—William Penn's *No Cross No Crown*. I like it immensely." Stephen Grellet, a French refugee of noble family who became one of the greatest ministers in the Society of Friends, records an experience on Long Island in 1795 which became the turning point in his life. He says, "I now took up again the works of William Penn and opened upon *No Cross No Crown*. The title alone reached my heart. I proceeded to read it, with the help of my dictionary, having to look for the meaning of nearly every word. I read it twice through in this manner. I had never met with anything of the kind; neither had I felt the Divine witness in me operating so powerfully before."

Readers will be surprised to discover how strongly their

interest is gripped by Penn's vigorous moralizing. His exhortations still retain their reaching power. Because of his exhuberant fluency, it has seemed worthwhile to prepare this abridgement of *No Cross No Crown,* preserving the essence which has not grown obsolete. It is as urgent today as when young William Penn concluded his pamphlet in the Tower of London "to live a humble, serious and self-denying life. So shall we be delivered from every snare, no sin shall gain us, no frowns scare us and the Truth shall be more abundantly exalted."

NO CROSS NO CROWN

Preface

COME, Reader, hearken to me awhile; I seek thy salvation; that's my plot; thou wilt forgive me. A Refiner
is come near thee, his grace hath appeared to thee; receive
its leaven, and it will change thee; his medicine, and it will
cure thee; he is as infallible as free; without money, and with
certainty. A touch of his garment did it of old; it will do it
still; his virtue is the same, it cannot be exhausted. He
turns vile things into things precious; for he maketh saints
out of sinners, and almost gods of men. What rests to us
then, that we must do, to be thus witnesses of his power
and love? This is the Crown; but where is the Cross?

Christ's Cross is Christ's way to Christ's Crown. This is the
subject of the following discourse, first writ during my con-
finement in the Tower of London, in the year 1668, now reprinted (1682) with enlargements that thou, Reader, mayest
be won to Christ; and if won already, brought nearer to him.
'Tis a path God in his everlasting kindness guided my feet
into, in the flower of my youth, when about two and twenty
years of age; then he took me by the hand and led me out
of the pleasures, vanities, and hopes of the world. I have
tasted of Christ's judgments, and of his mercies, and of the
world's frowns, and reproaches. I rejoice in my experience
and dedicate it to thy service in Christ.

To my country, and to the world of Christians I leave it.
May God, if he please, make it effectual to them all and
turn their hearts from that envy, hatred, and bitterness

1

they have one against another about worldly things (sacri-
ficing humanity and charity to ambition and covetousness,
for which they fill the earth with trouble and oppression)
that receiving the spirit of Christ into their hearts, the fruits
of which are love, peace, joy, temperance and patience,
brotherly kindness and charity, they may in body, soul, and
spirit, make a triple league against the world, the flesh,
and the devil, the only common enemies of mankind; and
having conquered them through a life of self-denial and
the power of the cross of Jesus, they may at last attain to
the eternal rest and kingdom of God.

So desireth, so prayeth,

Friendly Reader,

Thy fervent Christian friend,

WILLIAM PENN

Worminghurst in Sussex,
the 1st of the 6th month, 1682.

The Defection of Christendom

Though the knowledge and obedience of the doctrine of the cross of Christ be of infinite moment to the souls of men, for that is the only door to true Christianity, and that path the ancients ever trod to blessedness, yet with extreme affliction, let me say, it is so little understood, so much neglected and, what is worse, so bitterly contradicted by the vanity, superstition, and intemperance of professed Christians, that we must conclude that the generality of Christendom do miserably deceive and disappoint themselves in the great business of Christianity.

For, let us be never so tender and charitable in the survey of those nations that intitle themselves to any interest in the holy name of Christ, if we will be just too, we must needs acknowledge that after all the gracious advantages of light, the writings, labours, and martyrdom of his dear followers in all times, there seems very little left of Christianity but the name. The deity they truly worship is the god of the world. To him they bow with the whole powers of soul and sense. What shall we eat? What shall we drink? What shall we wear? And how shall we pass away our time? Which way may we accumulate wealth, increase our power, and enlarge our territories?

This miserable defection from primitive times, when the glory of Christianity was the purity of its professors, I cannot but call the second and worst part to the Jewish tragedy upon the blessed Saviour of mankind. For the Jews, from the power of ignorance and the extreme prejudice they were under to the unworldly way of his appearance, would not acknowledge him when he came, but for two or three

3

years persecuted, and finally crucified him in one day. But the false Christians' cruelty lasts longer: they have first, with Judas, professed him and then, for these many ages, most basely betrayed, persecuted, and crucified him, by a perpetual apostacy in manners from the self-denial and holiness of his doctrine, their lives giving the lie to their faith. If a man ask them, "Is Christ your Lord?" they will cry, "God forbid else. Yes, he is our Lord." "Very well; but do you keep his commandments?" "No. How should we?" "How then are you his disciples?" "It is impossible," say they. "What! would you have us keep his commandments? No man can." What! impossible to do that, without which Christ hath made it impossible to be a Christian? Is Christ unreasonable? That common apprehension—that they may be children of God, while in a state of disobedience to his holy commandments; disciples of Jesus, though they revolt from his cross; and members of his true church, that is without spot or wrinkle, notwithstanding their lives are full of spots and wrinkles—is, of all other deceptions upon themselves, the most pernicious to their eternal condition. For they are at peace in sin and under a security in their transgression. Their vain hope silences their convictions and overlays all tender motions to repentance, so that their mistake about their duty to God is as mischievous as their rebellion against him.

The Remedy

O Christendom! my soul most fervently prays that, after all thy lofty profession of Christ and his meek and holy religion, thy unsuitable and unchristlike life may not cast thee at that great assize of the world and lose thee so great salvation at last. Hear me once, I beseech thee. Can Christ be thy Lord and thou not obey him? Or, canst thou be his servant and never serve him?

Now, behold the remedy! an infallible cure, one of God's appointing, and that universal medicine which no malady could ever escape.

But thou wilt say, "What is Christ, and where to be found? And how received and applied in order to this mighty cure?" I tell thee then: first, that he is the great spiritual light of the world that lights every one that comes into the world, by which he manifests to them their deeds of darkness and wickedness, and reproves them for committing them. Secondly, that he is not far away from thee. Thou, like the inn of old, hast been full of other guests; thy affections have entertained other lovers, wherefore salvation is not yet come to thy house, or at least into it, though thou hast been often proffered it, and hast professed it long. But if he calls, if he knocks still, that is, if his light yet shines, if it reproves thee still, there is hope thy day is not over, nor is repentance yet hid from thine eyes. For this blessed work of reformation did Christ endue his apostles with his spirit and power. And truly, God so blessed the faithful labours of these poor mechanics, yet his great ambassadors to mankind, that in a few years many thousands, very strangers to the work of his spirit in their hearts, were inwardly struck and quickened to the word of life. Indeed, the glory of the Cross shined so conspicuously through the self-denial of their lives that daily bore it, that it struck the heathen with astonishment, and in a small time so shook their altars, discredited their oracles, struck the multitude, invaded the court and overcame their armies, that it led priests, magistrates, and generals in triumph after it, as the trophies of its power and victory.

And while this integrity dwelt with Christians, mighty

was the presence and invincible that power that attended them; it quenched fire, daunted lions, turned the edge of the sword, out-faced instruments of cruelty, convicted judges, and converted executioners. In fine, the ways their enemies took to destroy increased them. Their care was not how to sport away their precious time, but how to redeem it. For they, having with Moses seen him that is invisible and found that his loving-kindness was better than life, chose rather to sustain the afflictions of Christ's true pilgrims than to enjoy the pleasures of sin.

By this short draught of what Christendom was, thou mayst see, O Christendom, what thou art not, and consequently what thou oughtest to be. But how comes it that from a Christendom that was thus meek, merciful, self-denying, suffering, temperate, holy, just, and good, so like to Christ, whose name it bore, we find a Christendom now that is superstitious, idolatrous, persecuting, proud, passionate, envious, malicious, selfish, drunken, lascivious, unclean, lying, swearing, cursing, covetous, oppressing, defrauding, with all other abominations known in the earth?

I lay this down as the undoubted reason of this degeneracy, to wit, the inward disregard of thy mind to the light of Christ shining in thee. For as thy fear towards God, and holy abstinence from unrighteousness, was at first not taught by the precepts of men, but by that light and grace which revealed the most secret thoughts and purposes of thine heart, setting thy sins in order before thee and reproving thee for them, not suffering one unfruitful thought, word, or work of darkness to go unjudged, so, when thou didst begin to disregard that light and grace, to be careless of thy holy watch that was once set up in thine heart, and keptst not sentinel there, as formerly, for God's glory and thy own peace, the restless enemy of man's good quickly took advantage of this slackness, and often surprised thee with temptations, whose suitableness to thy inclinations made his conquest over thee not difficult.

Thou didst omit to take up Christ's holy yoke, to bear thy daily cross; thou wast careless of thy affections, and keptst no journal or check upon thy actions; but declinedst to audit accounts in thy own conscience with Christ thy light, whereby the holy fear decayed and love waxed cold, vanity abounded and duty became burdensome. Then up came formality, instead of the power of godliness; superstition in place of Christ's institution; the pure eye grew dim which repentance had opened, and those worldly pleasures that make such as love them forget God, began now to recover their old beauty and interest in thy affections and, from liking them, to be the study, care, and pleasure of thy life. Thus religion fell from experience to tradition, and worship, from power to form, from life to letter, so that a man may say with truth: thy condition is worse by thy religion, because thou art tempted to think thyself the better for it, and art not. For look! at what door thou wentest out, at that door thou must come in; and as letting fall and forbearing the daily cross lost thee, so taking up and enduring the daily cross must recover thee. Nothing short of this will do; for as it is sufficient so is it indispensable: no crown, but by the cross.

The Cross

The cross of Christ is a figurative speech, borrowed from the outward tree, or wooden cross, on which Christ submitted to the will of God in permitting him to suffer death at the hands of evil men. So that the cross mystical is that divine grace and power which crosseth the carnal wills of

7

men, and so may be justly termed the instrument of man's holy dying to the world and being made conformable to the will of God. The preaching of the cross, therefore, in primitive times was fitly called by Paul, that famous and skilful apostle in spiritual things, the power of God; though to them that perish, then, as now, foolishness, embraced by none, if they may be believed, but half-witted people of stingy and singular tempers, affected with the hypochondry and oppressed with the power of melancholy.

Well, but then where does this cross appear, and where must it be taken up? I answer, within, that is, in the heart and soul; for where the sin is, the cross must be. Custom in evil hath made it natural to men to do evil; and as the soul rules the body, so this corrupt nature sways the whole man; but still, 'tis all from within.

Experience teaches every son and daughter of Adam an assent to this; for the enemies' temptations are ever directed to the mind, which is within; if they take not, the soul sins not; if they are embraced, lust is presently conceived (that is, inordinate desires). Here is the very genealogy of sin.

But how and in what manner is the cross to be daily borne? The way, like the cross, is spiritual, that is, an inward submission of the soul to the will of God as it is manifested by the light of Christ in the consciences of men; the way of taking up the cross is an entire resignation of soul to the discoveries and requirings of it.

Self-Denial

What is the great work and business of the cross respecting man? I shall pursue the question with the best knowledge God hath given me in the experience of several years' discipleship.

The great work and business of the cross in man is self-denial, a word little understood by the world, but less embraced by it; yet it must be borne for all that. The Son of God is gone before us, and by the bitter cup he drank, and baptism he suffered, has left us an example, that we should follow his steps.

What is our cup and cross that we should drink and suffer? They are the denial and offering up of ourselves, by the same spirit, to do or suffer the will of God for his service and glory, which is the true life and obedience of the cross of Jesus, narrow still, but before, an unbeaten way. For when there was none to help, not one to give knowledge or direct the course of poor man's recovery, he came in the greatness of his love and strength, and though clothed with the infirmities of a mortal man, being within fortified by the almightiness of an immortal God, he travelled through all the straits and difficulties of humanity.

Oh, come! let us follow him, the most unwearied, the most victorious captain of our salvation, to whom all the great Alexanders and mighty Caesars of the world are less than the poorest soldier of their camps could be to them. They vanquished others, not themselves; Christ conquered self, that ever vanquished them. They advanced their empire by rapine and blood, but he by suffering and persuasion; he, never by compulsion, they always by force, prevailed. Misery and slavery followed all their victories; his brought greater freedom and felicity to those he overcame. In all they did, they sought to please themselves; in all he did, he aimed to please his Father.

'Tis this most perfect pattern of self-denial we must follow, to do which let us consider self-denial in its true distinction and extent. There is a lawful and an unlawful self, and both must be denied. The lawful self, which we are to deny, is that conveniency, ease, and enjoyment, and plenty, which in themselves are so far from being evils that they are the bounty and blessings of God to us: as husband, wife, child, house, land, reputation, liberty, and life itself— these are God's favours, which we may enjoy with lawful pleasure, and justly improve as our honest interest. But when God requires them, I say, when they are brought in competition with him, they must not be preferred; they must be denied. It is too much the sin of the best part of the world that they stick in the comforts of it, and 'tis lamentable to behold how their affections are bemired and entangled with their conveniences and accommodations in it.

But on the other hand it is not for nought that the disciples of Jesus deny themselves; and indeed, Christ himself had the eternal joy in his eye. 'Twas this recompense of reward, this eternal crown of righteousness that in every age has raised in the souls of the just an holy neglect, yea, contempt of the world.

The way of God is a way of faith, as dark to sense, as mortal to self. Speculation wont do, nor can refined notions enter. "They that do my will," says the blessed Jesus, "shall know of my doctrine." There is no room for instruction where lawful self is lord and not servant. For self can't receive it, that which should is oppressed by self, fearful, and dares not. Oh, what will my father or mother say? How will my husband use me? Or, finally, what will the magistrate do with me? For though I have a most powerful persuasion, and clear conviction upon my soul of this or that thing, yet considering how unmodish it is, what enemies it has, and how strange and singular I shall seem to them, I hope God will pity my weakness; if I sink, I am but flesh and blood; maybe hereafter he may better enable me; and there is time enough. Thus selfish, fearful man.

10

But deliberating is ever worst, for the soul loses in parley, the manifestation brings power with it. Never did God convince people, but upon submission he empowered them. They that want power are such as don't receive Christ in his convictions upon the soul; and such shall always want it. Tack about then, and hearken to the still voice in thy conscience; it tells thee thy sins and misery in them. It opens to thy soul some prospect of eternity.

Even in this world the righteous have the better of it, for they use the world without rebuke, because they don't abuse it. They see and bless the hand that feeds and clothes and preserves them. And as by beholding him in all his gifts, they don't adore them, but him; so the sweetness of his blessings that gives them, is an advantage such have upon those that see him not. Besides, in their increases they are not lifted up, nor in their adversities are they cast down. And why? Because they are moderated in the one, and comforted in the other, by his divine presence.

The Unlawful Self

I am now come to unlawful self, which, more or less, is the immediate concernment of much the greatest part of mankind. This unlawful self is twofold: first, that which relates to religious worship; secondly, that which concerns moral and civil conversation in the world. And they are both of infinite consequence to be considered by us. Christ drew off his disciples from the glory and worship of the outward temple, and instituted a more inward and spiritual cult. People must be acquainted with God as a spirit, consider him, and worship him as such. 'Tis not that bodily worship, nor these ceremonious services, in use among you now, that will serve or give acceptance with this God that

11

is a spirit. No, you must obey his spirit that strives with you, to gather you out of the evil of the world, that by bowing to the instructions and commands of his spirit in your own souls you may know what it is to worship him as a spirit where the soul is encloistered from sin. And this religious house the true followers of Christ carry about with them, who exempt not themselves from the conversation of the world, though they keep themselves from the evil of the world in their conversation. The cross of Christ truly overcomes the world, and leads a life of purity in the face of its allurements; they that bear it are not chained up for fear they should bite, nor locked up lest they should be stole away: no, they receive power from Christ to resist the evil, and not only not to offend others, but to love those that offend them, though not for offending them. What a world should we have if everybody, for fear of transgressing, should mew himself up within four walls! No such matter; the perfection of Christian life extends to every honest labour or traffic used among men. This severity is not the effect of Christ's free spirit, but a voluntary humility, trammels of men's own making, without prescription or reason. In all which, 'tis plain, they are their own law-givers and set their own rule, a constrained harshness, out of joint to the rest of the creation; for society is one great end of it, and not to be destroyed for fear of evil: but sin banished that spoils it, by steady reproof and a conspicuous example of tried virtue.

True Godliness. True godliness does not turn men out of the world, but enables them to live better in it, and excites their endeavours to mend it. Christians should keep the helm and guide the vessel to its port, not meanly steal out at the stern of the world, and leave those that are in it without a pilot, to be driven by the fury of evil times upon the rock or sand of ruin.

I must confess I am jealous of the salvation of my own species, having found mercy with my heavenly Father. I would have none deceive themselves to perdition, especially about religion, where people are most apt to take all for granted. The inward steady righteousness of Jesus is another thing than all the contrived devotion of poor superstitious man. And the soul that is awakened and preserved by his holy power and spirit lives to him in the way of his institution and worships him in his own spirit.

Retirement, 1694. Not that I would be thought to slight a true retirement, for I do not only acknowledge but admire solitude. Christ himself was an example of it; he loved and chose to frequent mountains, gardens, sea-sides. They are requisite to the growth of piety; and I reverence the virtue that seeks and uses it, wishing there were more of it in the world; but then it should be free, not constrained. What benefit to the mind to have it for a punishment and not a pleasure? Nay, I have long thought it an error among all sorts that use not monastic lives, that they have no retreats for the afflicted, the tempted, the solitary, and the devout, where they might undisturbedly wait upon God, pass through their religious exercises and, being thereby strengthened, might with more power over their own spirits enter into the business of the world again. For divine pleasures are found in a free solitude.

Worship

Not keeping to the manner of taking up the cross in worship, as well as other things, has been a great cause of

13

the troublesome superstition that is yet in the world. For men have no more brought their worship to the test than their sins; nay, less. But true worship can only come from a heart prepared by the Lord. He is a spirit, to whom words, place, and time, strictly considered, are improper. 'Tis the language of the soul God hears, nor can that speak but by the Spirit. So, though Christ taught his disciples to pray, they were, in some sort, disciples before he taught them. And his teaching them is not an argument that everybody must say that prayer, whether he can say it with the same heart, and under the same qualifications, as his poor disciples and followers did; but rather that, as they then, so we now are not to pray our own prayers, but his, that is, such as he enables us to make, as he enabled them then, in which the body ought never to go before the soul.

Preparation. But it may be asked, "How shall this preparation be obtained?" I answer, by waiting patiently, yet watchfully and intently, upon God. Here thou must not think thy own thoughts, nor speak thy own words, which indeed is the silence of the holy cross, but be sequestered from all the confused imaginations that are apt to throng and press upon the mind in those holy retirements. It is not for thee to think to overcome the Almighty by the most composed matter, cast into the aptest phrase. No, no. One groan, one sigh from a wounded soul, a heart touched with true remorse, excels and prevails with God. Wherefore stand still in thy mind, wait to feel something that is divine to prepare and dispose thee to worship truly and acceptably. And thus taking up the cross, and shutting the doors and windows of the soul against everything that would interrupt this attendance upon God, how pleasant soever the object be in itself, how lawful or needful at another season, the power of the Almighty will break in, his spirit will work and prepare the heart. 'Tis he that discovers and presses wants upon the soul, and when it cries it is he alone that supplies them. Petitions not springing from such a sense and preparation are formal and fictitious.

Inward Want. Those that are not sensible of inward wants, that have no fears nor terrors upon them, who feel no need of God's power to help them, nor of the light of his countenance to comfort them, what have such to do with prayer? They know not, they want not, they desire not what they pray for. They pray the will of God may be done, and do constantly their own. They ask for grace, and abuse that they have; they pray for the spirit, but resist it in themselves and scorn it in others. And in this inward insensibility they are as unable to praise God for what they have as to pray for what they have not. "Ye that fear the Lord, praise him; all ye the seed of Jacob, glorify him." Jacob was a plain man, of an upright heart; and they that are so are his seed. And though, with him, they may be as poor as worms in their own eyes, yet they receive power to wrestle with God, and prevail as he did.

Purification. If the touching of a dead or unclean beast made people unfit for temple or sacrifice till first sprinkled and sanctified, can we think so meanly of the worship that is instituted by Christ as that it should admit of unprepared and unsanctified offerings, or allow that those who either in thoughts, words, or deeds do daily touch that which is truly unclean can, without coming to the blood of Jesus that sprinkles the conscience from dead works, acceptably worship the pure God? 'Tis a downright contradiction to good sense: the unclean cannot acceptably worship that

15

which is holy; the impure that which is perfect. But we may by this see that worship is an inward work, that the soul must be touched and raised in its heavenly desires by the heavenly spirit, and that the true worship is in God's presence.

Oh, how is the better part of Christendom degenerated from David's example! He leaves not till he finds the Lord, that is, the comforts of his presence that brings the answer of love and peace to his soul. Nor was this his practice only, as a man more than ordinarily inspired; for he speaks of it as the way of worship then amongst the true people of God, the spiritual of that day.

Baptism. Christ expressly charged his disciples they should not stir from Jerusalem, but wait till they had received the baptism of the Holy Ghost in order to their preparation for the preaching of the glorious gospel of Christ to the world. And though that were an extraordinary effusion for an extraordinary work, yet the degree does not change the kind. On the contrary, if so much waiting and preparation by the Spirit was requisite to fit them to preach to man, some at least may be needful to fit us to speak to God.

It is not enough to know we want; but we should learn whether it be not sent us as a blessing—disappointments to the proud, losses to the covetous, and to the negligent, stripes; to remove these were to secure the destruction, not help the salvation, of the soul. But if those wants that are the subject of prayer were once agreed upon—though that be a mighty point, yet how to pray is still of greater moment than to pray; 'tis not the request, but the frame of the petitioner's spirit. The *what* may be proper, but the *how* defective.

16

Faith. 'Tis faith that animates prayer and presses it home. This is of highest moment on our part, and yet not in our power neither, for it is the gift of God: from him we must have it, and with one grain of it more work is done, more deliverance is wrought, and more goodness and mercy received, than by all the runnings, and willings, and toilings of man, with his inventions and bodily exercises. Which, duly weighed, will easily spell out the meaning that so much worship should bring so little profit to the world as we see it does; namely, true faith is lost.

Can the minister then preach without faith? No, and much less can any man pray to purpose without faith. For worship is the supreme act of man's life, and whatever is necessary to inferior acts, must not be wanting there. But some may say, "What is this faith that is so necessary to worship and that gives it such acceptance with God and returns that benefit to men?" I say, it is a holy resignation to God and confidence in him, which gives sure evidence to the soul of the things not yet seen, and a general sense and taste of the substance of those things that are hoped for.

Pride

Having thus discharged my conscience against that part of unlawful self that fain would be a Christian whilst a plain stranger to the cross of Christ, and in that briefly discovered what is true worship, I shall now more largely prosecute that other part of unlawful self which fills the study, care, and conversation of the world—pride, avarice, and luxury, from whence all other mischiefs daily flow.

Pride is an excess of self-love, joined with an undervaluing of others, and a desire of dominion over them: the most troublesome thing in the world. There are four things by

17

which it hath made itself best known to mankind, the consequences of which have brought an equal misery to its evil. The first is an inordinate pursuit of knowledge. The second, an ambitious seeking and craving after power. The third, an extreme desire of personal respect and deference. The last excess is that of worldly furniture and ornaments.

To the first, 'tis plain that an inordinate desire of knowledge introduced man's misery and brought a universal lapse from the glory of his primitive estate. Adam would needs be wiser than God had made him. It did not serve his turn to know his Creator and give him holy homage, but he must be as wise as God too. This unwarrantable search, and as foolish as unjust ambition, made him unworthy of the blessings he received from God. This drives him out of paradise; and instead of being lord of the whole world, Adam becomes the wretchedest vagabond of the earth.

Strange that instead of being as gods, Adam and Eve should fall below the very beasts. The lamentable consequence of this great defection has been an exchange of innocency for guilt, and a paradise for a wilderness. But, which is yet worse, in this state they had got another god than the only true and living God; and he that had enticed them to all this mischief furnished them with a vain knowledge and pernicious wisdom, the skill of lies, evasions, and excuses. They had lost their plainness and sincerity; and from an upright heart, the image in which God had made man, he became a crooked, twining, twisting serpent—the image of that unrighteous spirit to whose temptations he yielded up with his obedience his paradisical happiness.

Nor is this limited to Adam; for all who have fallen short of the glory of God have sinned against that divine light of knowledge which God has given them. They have grieved his spirit, and that dismal sentence has been executed: when thou doest the thing which thou oughtest not to do, thou shalt no more enjoy the comforts of the peace of my spirit. And man becomes as one cold and benumbed, insensible of the love of God, of the light and joy of his countenance, and of the evidence of a good conscience, and of the co-witnessing and approbation of God's Holy Spirit.

So that fallen Adam's knowledge of God stood no more in a daily experience of the love and work of God in his soul, but in a notion of what he once did know and experience, which being not the true and living wisdom that is from above, but a mere picture, it preserves not man in purity, but puffs up, makes people proud, high-minded, and impatient of contradiction. This was the state of the apostate Jews before Christ came, and has been the condition of apostate Christians ever since he came: their religion standing either in what they once knew of the work of God in themselves, and which they revolted from, or in an historical belief and an imaginary conception and paraphrase upon the experiences and prophecies of such holy men and women of God as in all ages have deserved the style and character of his true children.

As such a knowledge of God cannot be true, so by experience we find that it ever brings forth the quite contrary fruits to the true wisdom. For as this is first pure, then peaceable, then gentle, and easy to be entreated, so the knowledge of degenerated and unmortified men is impure, unpeaceable, cross, and hard to be entreated, perverse, and persecuting, jealous that any should be better than they, and hating and abusing those that are. For they could not bear true vision when it came to visit them, and entertained the messengers of their peace as if they had been wolves and tigers. Yet, 'tis remarkable, the false prophets, the great engineers against the true ones, were ever sure to persecute them as false, and by their interest with earthly princes, or the poor seduced multitude, made them the instruments of malice.

The true knowledge came with the joy of angels, singing, "Peace to the earth and good will towards men." The false knowledge entertained the message with calumnies: Christ must needs be an impostor. They stoned him, and frequently sought to kill him, which at last they accomplished. But what was their motive to it? Why! he cried out against their hypocrisy, the honour they sought of men. To be short, they give the reason themselves in these words: "If we take not some course with him, the people will follow him," that is, he will take away our credit with the people; they will adhere to him, and desert us; and so we shall lose our power and reputation with the multitude. And, the truth is, he came to level their honour, and by his grace to bring the people to that inward knowledge of God which they, by transgression, were departed from, that so they might see the deceitfulness of their blind guides, who, by their vain traditions, had made void the righteousness of the law. The apostle goes further and affirms, "that the world by wisdom knew not God," that is, it was so far from a help that it was a hindrance to the true knowledge of God.

Well! but what has been the success of those ages that followed the apostolical? any whit better? Not one jot. They have exceeded them, as with their pretences to greater knowledge, so in their degeneracy from the true Christian life; for though they had a more excellent pattern than the Jews, to whom God spoke by Moses his servant, he speaking to the Christians by his beloved Son, the express image of his own substance, the perfection of all meekness and humility, and though they seemed addicted to nothing more than an adoration of his name, yet so great was their defection from the inward power and life of Christianity in the soul that their respect was little more than formal and ceremonious.

Yet about the great and weighty things of the Christian law, as love, meekness, and self-denial, they degenerated and grew high-minded, proud boasters, without natural affection, curious and controversial, ever perplexing the church with doubtful and dubious questions, filling the people with disputations, strife, and wrangling, drawing them into parties, till at last they fell into blood, as if they had been the worse for being once Christians.

Oh, the miserable state of these pretended Christians! that instead of Christ's and his apostles' doctrine of loving enemies and blessing them that curse them, they should teach the people, under the notion of Christian zeal, most inhumanly to butcher one another; and instead of suffering their own blood to be shed for the testimony of Jesus, they should shed the blood of the witnesses of Jesus for heretics. How it is in our own age, I leave to the experience of the living; yet there is one demonstration that can hardly fail us: the people are not converted but debauched to a degree that time will not allow us an example.

The way of recovery is to come to an experience of the divine work in the soul, to obtain which be diligent to obey the grace that appears in thy own soul, O man! that turns thee out of the broad way into the narrow way. Thou must not look at thy tempter, but at thy preserver; retire to thy solitudes; be a chaste pilgrim in this evil world; and thus thou wilt arrive to the knowledge of God and Christ, a well-grounded assurance from what a man feels and knows within himself.

Power

But let us see the next most common, eminent, and mischievous effect of this evil. Pride does extremely crave power, than which not one thing has proved more troublesome and destructive to mankind. I need not labour myself much in evidence of this, since most of the wars of nations, depopulation of kingdoms, ruin of cities, with the slavery and misery that have followed, both our own experience and unquestionable histories acquaint us to have been the effect of ambition, which is the lust of pride after power.

If we look abroad into remoter parts of the world, we shall rarely hear of wars, but in Christendom, rarely of peace. A very trifle is too often made a ground of quarrel here; nor can any league be so sacred or inviolable that arts shall not be used to evade and dissolve it to increase dominion. No matter who, nor how many, are slain, made widows and orphans, or lose their estates and livelihoods, what countries are ruined, what towns and cities spoiled, if by all these things the ambitious can but arrive at their ends.

But ambition does not only dwell in courts and senates; 'tis too natural to every private breast to strain for power. We daily see how much men labour their utmost wit and interest to be great; to get higher places, or greater titles than they have, that they may look bigger and be more acknowledged; take place of their former equals and so equal those that were once their superiors; compel friends and be revenged on enemies. This makes Christianity so little loved of worldly men—it's kingdom is not of this world, and though they may speak it fair, 'tis the world they love—that without uncharitableness we may truly say, people profess Christianity but they follow the world. Great is their peace who know a limit to their ambitious minds, that are not careful to be great but, being great, are humble, and do good. Such keep their wits with their consciences, and with an even mind can at all times measure the uneven world.

Respect

The third evil effect of pride is an excessive desire of personal honour and respect. Pride loves power that she might have homage and that every one may give her honour. And the practice of the world, even in our own age, will tell us that not striking a flag and not saluting certain ports or garrisons—yea, less things—have given rise to mighty wars between states, to the expense of much treasure but more blood, also the envy, quarrels, and mischiefs that have happened among private persons upon conceit of not being respected to their degree or quality among men, with hat, knee, or title, duels and murders not a few.

I was once myself in France, which was before I professed the communion I am now of, set upon about eleven at night, as I was walking to my lodging, by a person that waylaid me with his naked sword in his hand, who demanded satisfaction of me for taking no notice of him at a time when he civilly saluted me with his hat; though the truth was, I saw him not when he did it. I will suppose he had killed me, for he made several passes at me, or I in my defence had killed him, when I disarmed him. I ask any man of understanding or conscience, if the whole ceremony were worth the life of one man, considering the dignity of the nature and the importance of the life of man both with reference to God his creator, himself, and the benefit of civil society?

But the truth is, the world is as much out of the way as to true honour and respect as in other things. Did men know a true Christian state and the honour that comes from above, they would not covet these very vanities, much less insist upon them.

And here give me leave to set down the reasons why I, and the people with whom I walk in religious society, have declined several worldly customs and fashions of respect, much in request at this time of day. And I beseech thee, reader, to lay aside all prejudice and scorn and, with the meekness and inquiry of a sober and discreet mind, read and weigh what may be here alleged in our defence. If we are mistaken, rather pity and inform, than despise and abuse, our simplicity.

The first and most pressing motive upon our spirits to decline the practice of these present customs of pulling off the hat, bowing the body or knee, and giving people gaudy titles and epithets in our salutations and addresses, was that savour, sight, and sense that God has given us of the Christian world's apostasy from him. He was a swift witness against every evil thought and every unfruitful work, and we were not offended at his righteous judgments. Now it was that a grand inquest came upon our whole life; every word, thought, and deed was brought to judgment; the root examined and its tendency considered. In the fear and presence of the all-seeing just God, the present honours and respect of the world, among other things, became burdensome to us; we saw that they grew in the night-time and came from an ill root, that they only delighted a vain and ill mind, and that much pride and folly were in them.

Though we easily foresaw the storms of reproach that would fall upon us for our refusing to practise them, yet we were so far from being shaken in our judgment that it abundantly confirmed our sense of them. For so exalted a thing is man that it was greater heresy and blasphemy to refuse him the homage of the hat and his usual titles of honour, to deny to pledge his healths, or play with him at cards and dice, than any other principle we maintained.

To say that we strain at small things, which becomes not people of so fair pretensions to liberty and freedom of spirit, I answer with meekness, truth, and sobriety: first, nothing is small that God makes matter of conscience to do or to leave undone. Next, as little as they are objected upon us, they are much set by; so greatly, as for our not giving them, to be beaten, imprisoned and refused justice. So if we had wanted a proof of the truth of our inward belief and judgment, the very practice of them that opposed it would have abundantly confirmed us. But we only passively let fall the practice of what we believe is vain and unchristian; in which we are negative to forms.

The world is so set upon the ceremonious part and outside of things that it has well beseemed the wisdom of God in all ages to bring forth his dispensations with very different appearances to their settled customs, thereby contradicting human inventions and proving the integrity of his confessors. Nay it is a test upon the world: it tries what patience, kindness, sobriety, and moderation they have. If the rough and homely outside of truth stumble not their minds from the reception of it, whose beauty is within, it makes a great discovery upon them. For he who refuses a precious jewel because it is presented in a plain box will never esteem it to its value, nor set his heart upon keeping it. Therefore I call it a test, because it shows where the hearts and affections of people stick, after all their great pretences to more excellent things. But there is a hidden treasure in it: it inures us to reproach; it learns us to despise the false reputation of the world; and finally, with a Christian meekness and patience, to overcome their injuries and reproaches. It weans thee off thy familiars; for by being slighted of them as a ninney, a fool, a frantic, thou art delivered from a greater temptation, and that is the power and influence of their worldly conversation. And last of all, it lists thee of the company of the blessed, mocked, persecuted Jesus, to fight under his banner.

I shall conclude this with one passage more, and that is a very large, plain, and pertinent one: "Honour all men, and love the brotherhood": that is, love is above honour, and that is reserved for the brotherhood. But honour, that is, esteem and regard, thou owest to all men, and if all, then thy inferiors. But why for all men? Because they are the creation of God, and the noblest part of his creation too; they are also thy own kind. Be natural, and assist them with what thou canst; be ready to perform any real respect, and yield them any good or countenance thou canst.

We are, we declare to the whole world, for true honour and respect: we honour the king, our parents, our masters, our magistrates, our landlords, one another—yea, all men, after God's way. Honour was from the beginning, but hat-respects and most titles are of late; there was true honour before hats or titles, and true honour stands not in them. And that which ever was the way to express true honour is the best way still. They that endure faithful in that which they are convinced God requires of them, though against the gain and humour of the world and themselves too, they shall find a blessed recompense in the end. However, Christians are not so ill bred as the world thinks, for they show respect too, but the difference lies in the nature of the respect they perform, and the reasons of it.

The world's respect is an empty ceremony; the Christian's

26

is a solid thing, for fine apparel, empty titles, or large revenues are the world's motives, but the Christian's motive is the sense of his duty in God's sight: first, to parents and magistrates; and then to inferior relations; and lastly, to all people, according to their virtue, wisdom, and piety. We shall easily grant our honour, as our religion is more hidden. Our plainness is odd, uncouth, and goes mightily against the grain; but so does Christianity too, and that for the same reasons. Oh, that Christians would look upon themselves with the glass of righteousness, that which tells true and gives them an exact knowledge of themselves! And then let them examine what, of them and about them agrees with Christ's doctrine and life.

Thou for You

There is another piece of our non-conformity to the world that renders us very clownish to the breeding of it, and that is our plain and homely speech, using "Thou" for "You," and that without difference or respect to persons. Words of themselves are but as so many marks set and employed for necessary and intelligible means, whereby men may understandingly express their minds and conceptions to each other, from whence comes society. It seems the word "Thou" looked too lean and thin a respect to proud emperors; and therefore some, bigger than they should be, would have a style suitable to their own ambition, a ground we cannot build our practice on, for what begun it only loves it still.

But some will tell us: custom should rule us; and that is against us. But it is as easily answered that though in things reasonable or indifferent custom is obliging or harmless, yet in things unreasonable or unlawful she has no authority.

27

To use the same word for One and Many, when there are two, and that only to please a proud and haughty humour in man, is not reasonable in our sense, which, we hope, is Christian, though not modish. But I would not have thee think it is a mere Thou or title, nakedly in themselves, we boggle at, but the esteem and value the vain minds of men do put upon them, that constrains us to testify so steadily against them.

Wherefore let me beseech thee, reader, to consider the foregoing reasons, which were mostly given me from the Lord, in that time when my condescension to these fashions would have been purchased at almost any rate; but the certain sense I had of their contrariety to the meek and self-denying life of holy Jesus required my disuse of them and faithful testimony against them. It was extreme irksome to me to decline and expose myself, but I dared not gratify that mind in myself or others.

Rank and Beauty

But pride stops not here. She excites people to an excessive value and care of their persons; they must have great and punctual attendance, stately furniture, rich and exact apparel, especially if they have any pretence either to blood or beauty. The one has raised many quarrels among men; and the other among women, and men too often, for their sakes, and at their excitements.

What a pudder has this noble blood made in the world! Whose father or mother, great-grandfather, or great-grandmother, was best descended or allied? What stock, or what clan, they came of? Methinks, nothing of man's folly has less show of reason to palliate it. This is like being the true church because old, not because good, for families to

28

be noble by being old, and not by being virtuous. No such matter! To be descended of wealth and titles fills no man's head with brains, nor heart with truth: those qualities come from a higher cause.

But I must grant that the condition of our great men is much to be preferred to the ranks of inferior people for they have more power to do good, and, if their hearts be equal to their ability, they are blessings to the people of any country. They have more time to observe the actions of other nations; to travel; and view the laws, customs and interests of other countries; and to bring home whatsoever is worthy and imitable. And, to say true, if there be any advantage in such descent, 'tis not from blood, but education, for blood has no intelligence in it, and is often spurious and uncertain; but education has a mighty influence and strong bias upon the affections and actions of men.

But personal pride ends not in nobility of blood; it leads folks to a fond value of their persons, especially if they have any pretence to shape or beauty. It would abate their folly if they could find in their hearts to spare but half the time to think of God which they most prodigally spend in washing, perfuming, painting, patching, attiring, and dressing. In these things they are precise and very artificial, and for cost they spare not; but which aggravates the evil—the pride of one might comfortably supply the need of ten. No age can better tell us the sad effects of this sort of pride than this we live in; as, how excessive wanton, so how fatal it has been to the sobriety, virtue, peace, and health of families in this kingdom.

Human Relations

A proud man is a kind of glutton upon himself, and how troublesome a companion, ever positive and controlling and, if you yield not, insolent and quarrelsome; yet at the upshot of the matter, cowardly; but if strongest, cruel! Pride destroys the nature of relations; it turns love into fear, and makes the wife a servant, and the children and servants, slaves. The proud man makes an ill neighbor too, for he is an enemy to hospitality; he despises to receive kindness, because he would show none, nor be thought to need it. He values other men as we do cattle, for their service only; and, if he could, would use them so; but, as it happens, the number and force are unequal.

But a proud man in power is very mischievous; for his pride is the more dangerous by his greatness, since from ambition in private men it becomes tyranny in him. The men of this temper would have nothing thought amiss they do; no, they will rather choose to perish obstinately than, by acknowledging, yield away the reputation of better judging to inferiors; though it were their prudence to do so. And, indeed, 'tis all the satisfaction that proud great men make to the world for the miseries they often bring upon it that, first or last, they leave their real interest to follow some one excess of humour, and are almost ever destroyed by it. This is the end pride gives proud men and the ruin it brings upon them, after it has punished others by them.

But above all things, pride is intolerable in men pretending to religion. For what should pride do with religion, that rebukes it? or ambition with ministers, whose very office is humility? But alas, when all is done, what folly, as well as irreligion, is there in pride! What crosses can it hinder, what disappointments help, or harm frustrate? It delivers not from the common stroke; sickness disfigures; pain misshapes; and death ends the proud man's fabric. Six foot of cold earth bounds his big thoughts.

Wealth

I am come to the second part of this discourse, which is avarice, or covetousness, an epidemical and a raging distemper in the world, attended with all the mischiefs that can make men miserable in themselves, and in society. Oh, that this thing was better considered! For by not being so observable nor obnoxious to the law as other vices are, there is more danger for want of that check.

'Tis plain that most people strive not for substance, but wealth. Some there be that love it strongly, and spend it liberally when they have got it. Though this be sinful, yet 'tis more commendable than to love money for money's sake. That is one of the basest passions the mind of man can be captivated by: a greater and more soul-defiling one there is not in the catalogue of concupiscence. Which should quicken people into a serious examination how far this temptation hath entered them, because the steps it maketh into the mind are almost insensible, which makes the danger greater. Do we not see how early they rise, how late they go to bed, how full of the shop, the warehouse, the custom-house, of bills, bonds, charter-parties, they are, running up and down as if it were to save the life of a condemned innocent?

To conclude, wealth is an enemy to government in magistrates, for it tends to corruption; and the great reason why some have too little, and so are forced to drudge like slaves to feed their families and keep their chin above water, is because the rich hold hard, to be richer and covet more, which dries up the little streams of profit from smaller folks. There should be a standard, both as to the quantity and time of traffic, and then the trade of the master should be shared amongst his servants that deserve it. This were both to help the young to get their livelihood, and to give the old time to think of leaving this world well, in which they have been so busy.

Covetousness has caused destructive feuds in families; it betrays friendship, and where money masters the mind it extinguishes all love to better things. The covetous man is like the poles, always cold: an enemy to the state, for he spirits their money away; a disease to the body politic, for he obstructs the circulation of the blood, and ought to be removed by a purge of the law. 'Twas upon these rich men that Christ pronounced his woe, saying: "Woe unto you that are rich, for ye have received your consolation here." What! none in the heavens? No, unless you become willing to be poor men, can resign all, live loose to the world, have it at arm's end, yea, underfoot, a servant, and not a master.

Luxury

I am now come to the other extreme and that is luxury, an excessive indulgence of self in ease and pleasure. A disease as epidemical as killing, it creeps into all stations and ranks of men, the poorest often exceeding their ability to indulge their appetite, and the rich frequently wallowing in those things that please their eye and flesh. Sumptuous apparel, rich unguents, delicate washes, stately furniture, costly cookery, and such diversions as balls, masques, musics, plays, romances, which are the delight and entertainment of the times, belong not to the holy path of Jesus and his true disciples. Oh, that the sons and daughters of men would consider how cruel they are to his creatures, how lavish of their lives and virtue, how thankless for them! Forgetting the giver, and abusing the gift, they lose tenderness, and forget duty, being swallowed up of voluptuousness.

Nor is it otherwise with recreations, as they call them, for these are nearly joined. Man was made a noble, rational, grave creature; his pleasure stood in his duty and in using the creation with true temperance and godly indifference. If the recreations of the age were as pleasant and necessary as they are said to be, unhappy then would Adam and Eve have been, that never knew them. Then the best recreations were to serve God, be just, follow their vocations, mind their flocks, do good, exercise their bodies in such practices as might be suitable to gravity, temperance, and virtue.

Nay, such are the remains of innocence among some Moors and Indians to our times that if a Christian, though he must be an odd one, fling out a filthy word, it's customary with them, by way of moral, to bring him water to purge his mouth. If, then, the distinguishing mark between the disciples of Jesus and those of the world is that one minds God's kingdom and that the other minds eating, drinking, apparel, and the affairs of the world, be you entreated for your souls' sake to reflect a while upon yourselves, what care and cost you are at, of time and money, what buying and selling, what dealing and chaffering, what writing and posting, what noise, hurry, bustle and confusion, what little contrivances, what rising early, going to bed late, what expense of precious time is there about things that perish. And is not the world, this fading world, writ upon every face?

That which further manifests the unlawfulness of these numerous fashions and recreations is that they are either the inventions of vain, idle, and wanton minds to gratify their own sensualities or the contrivances of indigent and impoverished wits, who make it the next way for their maintenance, in both which respects, and upon both which considerations, they ought to be detested as diverting from more lawful, more serviceable, and more necessary employments.

How many pieces of riband, and what feathers, lace-bands, and the like, did Adam and Eve wear in paradise, or out of it? What rich embroideries, silks, and points had Abel, Enoch, Noah, and good old Abraham? Did Eve, Sarah, Susannah, Elizabeth, and the Virgin Mary use to curl, powder, patch, paint, wear false locks of strange colors, rich points, trimmings, laced gowns, embroidered petticoats, shoes and slipslaps laced with silk or silver lace, and ruffled like pigeons' feet, with several yards, if not pieces of ribands? How many plays did Jesus Christ and his apostles recreate themselves at?

I know I am coming to encounter the most plausible objection men are used to urge, when driven to a pinch: "But how shall those many families subsist, whose livelihood depends upon such fashions and recreations as you so earnestly decry?" I answer: It is a bad argument to plead for the commission of the least evil, that never so great a good may come of it. If you and they have made wickedness your pleasure and your profit, be ye content that it should be your grief and punishment, till the one can learn to be without such vanity, and the others have found out more honest employments.

'Tis the vanity of the few great ones that makes so much toil for the many small. Would men learn to be contented with few things, such as are necessary and convenient, all things might be at a cheaper rate, and men might live for little. If the landlords had less lusts to satisfy, the tenants might have less rent to pay, and turn from poor to rich, whereby they might be able to find more honest and domestic employments for their children than turning shifters and living by their wits, which is but a better word for their sins. And if the report of the more intelligent in husbandry be credible, lands are generally improvable; and were there more hands about more lawful and serviceable manufactures, they would be cheaper, and greater vent might be made by which a benefit would redound to the world in general. Nay, the burden lies the heavier upon the laborious country, that so many hands and shoulders, as have the lust-caterers of the cities, should be wanting to the plough and the useful husbandry.

Let such of those vanity-hucksters as have got sufficient be contented to retreat and spend it more honestly than they have got it; and such as really are poor be rather helped to better callings: this were more prudent, nay, Christian, than to consume money upon such foolish toys and fopperies. We cannot, we dare not, square our conversation by the world's: no, but by our exceeding plainness to testify against such extravagant vanity.

I know that some are ready further to object: "Hath God given us these enjoyments on purpose to damn us if we use them?" I answer that what God made was good, but in the whole catalogue the scriptures give, I never found the attires, recreations, and way of living, so much in request with the called Christians of these times; no, certainly. God created man a holy, wise, sober, grave, and reasonable creature, fit to govern himself and the world.

The Public Good

Every one that pretends to seriousness ought to suspect himself, as having been too forward to help on the excess, for every man should be so wise as to deny himself the use of such indifferent enjoyments as cannot be used by him without too manifest an encouragement to his neighbor's folly. People are not to weigh their private satisfactions more than a public good. Wherefore it is both reasonable and incumbent on all to make only such things necessary as tend to life and godliness, and to employ their freedom with most advantage to their neighbors.

If men and women were but thus adorned, impudence would soon receive a check, virtue would be in credit, and excess not dare show its face; then primitive innocency and plainness would come back again, and that plain-hearted, downright, harmless life would be restored of not much caring what we should eat, drink, or put on.

The temperance I plead for is not only religiously but politically good; 'tis the interest of good government to curb and rebuke excesses; it prevents many mischiefs; luxury brings effeminacy, laziness, poverty, and misery, but temperance preserves the land. It keeps out foreign vanities and improves our own commodities: now we are their debtors, then they would be debtors to us for our native manufactures. We cannot but loudly call upon the generality of the times and testify both by our life and doctrine against abuses if possibly any may be weaned from their folly.

When people have first learned to fear, worship and obey their Creator, when the pale faces are more commiserated, the pinched bellies relieved, and naked backs clothed, when the famished poor, the distressed widow, and helpless orphan, God's works, and your fellow creatures, are provided for, then, I say, if then, it will be early enough for you to plead the indifferency of your pleasures. But that the sweat and tedious labour of the husbandmen, early and late, cold and hot, wet and dry, should be converted into the pleasure, ease, and pastime of a small number of men; that the cart, the plough, the thrash, should be in that continual severity laid upon nineteen parts of the land to feed the inordinate lusts and delicious appetites of the twentieth, is so far from the appointment of the great Governor of the world, and God of the spirits of all flesh, that to imagine such horrible injustice as the effects of his determinations, and not the intemperance of men, were wretched and blasphemous, especially since God hath made the sons of men but stewards to each other's exigencies and relief.

I therefore humbly offer an address to the serious consideration of the civil magistrate, that if the money which is expended in every parish in vain fashions could be collected in a public stock, there might be reparation to the broken tenants, work-houses for the able, and almshouses for the aged and impotent. Then should we have no beggars in the land, the cry of the widow and the orphan would cease, nay, the exchequer's needs, on just emergencies, might be supplied by such a bank: it would be a noble example of gravity and temperance to foreign states, and an unspeakable benefit to ourselves at home.

Alas! why should men need persuasions to what their own felicity so necessarily leads them to? This vanity and excess are acted under a profession of the self-denying religion of Jesus, whose life and doctrine are a perpetual reproach to the most of Christians. For he (blessed man) was humble, but they are proud; he forgiving, they revengeful; he meek, they fierce; he plain, they gaudy; he abstemious, they lux-

37

urious; he chaste, they lascivious; he a pilgrim on earth, they citizens of the world: in fine, he was meanly born, poorly attended, and obscurely brought up; he lived despised, and died hated of the men of his own nation. If you will listen to the light and grace that comes by him and which he has given to all people, and square your thoughts, words, and deeds thereby, and live soberly and godly, then may you with confidence look for the blessed hope, and joyful coming, and glorious appearing of the great God, and our Saviour Jesus Christ.

O Lord God! Thou lovest holiness, and purity is thy delight in the earth. Wherefore, I pray thee, make an end of sin, and finish transgression, and bring in the everlasting righteousness to the souls of men, that thy poor creation may be delivered from the bondage it groans under, and the earth enjoy her sabbath again, that thy great name may be lifted up in all nations, and thy salvation renowned to the ends of the world.

BARCLAY IN BRIEF

AN ABBREVIATION OF ROBERT BARCLAY'S
Apology for the True Christian Divinity

By
ELEANORE PRICE MATHER

PENDLE HILL PAMPHLET 28

INTRODUCTION

R. B. Unto the Friendly Reader Wisheth Salvation

THIS timeless greeting comes to us from the opening pages of Robert Barclay's *Apology for the True Christian Divinity*, the book which more clearly and comprehensively than any other formulates the doctrine held by the Society of Friends. For while George Fox and his early followers testified to the Seed of Light within the soul of every man, and pointed the way to group organization and behavior, it was left to Barclay to round these beliefs into a religious system and present them as such to the world.

For this work he was well qualified. Born 1648 near the shores of the Firth of Moray, he inherited from his native highland soil that talent for theological disputation peculiar to the Scottish people. This gift was sharpened by early training in Presbyterian schools of the neighborhood, and broadened by later study in Paris where he came in contact with the Roman Catholic faith and for a time seriously considered making it his own. At the age of eighteen, however, he joined the Society of Friends, following the example of his father, David Barclay, the doughty Scottish Laird whom Whittier celebrated in his *Barclay of Ury*.

Like William Penn and Isaac Penington, Robert Barclay was a well-educated aristocrat who showed his freedom of spirit by embracing what was primarily a religion of the poor. To these men fell the task of putting into scholarly terms the principles of the new faith—a faith which, though nominally new, was looked on by its adherents as a reaffirmation of primitive Christianity. And they did more than this. They used their legal knowledge to aid fellow-members

41

who were hailed before magistrates for conscience sake, they opened their purses to support the families of those who were fined or imprisoned, they shared the hardships of the dank and filthy dungeons of seventeenth century England and Scotland.

These imprisonments were a self-assumed discipline with Robert Barclay. He could have easily obtained release, for through his mother, Catherine Gordon, he was related to the royal house of Stuart, and also to certain rulers on the European Continent. Among these was Princess Elizabeth of the Palatinate, a woman eager in mind and spirit and a friend of the philosopher Descartes. With this cousin he exchanged a series of letters which reveal his sympathy and spiritual insight. He saw her several times during his religious journeys on the Continent, and on one of these visits was accompanied by George Fox and William Penn. This is the only record we have of the coming together of the three great leaders. Unlike Fox and Penn, Barclay never came in person to the New World, but by his kinsman, James II, with whom he had considerable influence, he was appointed governor of East Jersey, a position which he filled by deputy from 1682-1688.

His domestic life was tranquil and happy. He married Christian Molleson, a Quakeress of Aberdeen, to whom he wrote in the days of their courtship, "The love of thy converse, the desire of thy friendship, the sympathy of thy way, and the meekness of thy spirit, have often, as thou mayest have observed, occasioned me to take frequent opportunity to have the benefit of thy company . . . but beyond and before all I can say, in the fear of the Lord, that I have received a charge from Him to love thee." They had seven children. Certain of Robert Barclay's descendants have been noted for their literary work, but none of them attained his prominence. In 1690, at the comparatively early age of forty-one, he died at the Manor of Ury, his father's estate near Aberdeen. We know from the testimony of his friends that he was in all things brave and gentle and true, a lover of peace, but never hesitant to take up the weapons of spiritual warfare to defend the faith as it was revealed to him. At the time of his death George Fox consoled Christian Barclay with these words: "Thou and thy family may rejoice that thou hadst such an offering to offer up unto the Lord."

No picture or likeness of him is known to us. His works are his monument. These were collected after his death and published under the apt title of *Truth Triumphant*. In spite of his many writings he may fitly be said to be a man of one book, and that book the *Apology for the True Christian Divinity*. For though his *Catechism and Confession of Faith* went into numerous European and American editions, and his *Anarchy of the Ranters* was read extensively by contemporaries, to subsequent generations he has always been known as the "Apologist."

For the *Apology* holds a place unique in the history of the Society of Friends. It is the supreme declaration of Quaker belief, organized and set forth by a man who, up to the nineteenth century, remained Quakerism's only theologian. First written in Latin and published in Amsterdam, 1676, it has been translated and published in English, Low Dutch, German, French, Spanish, Danish, and part of it in Arabic, passing into many editions and easily outselling any other book dealing with Quaker thought.

Our grandfathers read it widely and it was universally taught in Friends' Schools. But in the past generation it has fallen into disuse, and though every Friends' library contains the *Apology*, scarcely a Quaker under thirty has read it. This is unfortunate, because Barclay has perhaps a greater message for us today than he had for those earlier generations who knew him so well.

For this reason we have prepared this condensation which we hope will appeal to minds trained to the brevity of modern journalism, and by which readers may obtain in capsule form the essence of a timeless spiritual truth.

But in taking Barclay down from the shelf we shall meet with certain difficulties. Probably the most obvious is his use of the term "natural" man to mean sinful man. We find this hard to understand because we are inheritors of Rousseau's belief in the natural goodness of man, and of the more recent schools of psychology which emphasize the value of expressing the self by the gratification of natural impulses. Consequently we have come to look on the word "natural" as being almost a synonym for good.

The modern point of view and Barclay have this much in common: they both presuppose a primitive state of happiness and wish to regain it. The philosophers who exalted the natural goodness of man envisioned a physical return to the joyous freedom of woodland glades and a mingling with unspoiled aborigines. The picture of a world-weary sophisticate sporting side by side with the noble savage is pleasant to contemplate, particularly from the safe distance of an eighteenth century Parisian salon. But cold fact has revealed the aborigines to be frequently more savage than noble, and so bound by primitive taboos as to have infinitely less freedom than does the civilized man.

The plain truth of the matter is that it is useless to say, "Let's be primitive." The human race has long since passed from the Garden of Innocence. Try as we may we are not Adam before the Fall, much less the simple animal which some psychologists would have us be.

44

Though certain benefits have accrued to us through these attitudes toward the problem of human life they do not, in and of themselves, answer that problem. The trouble is that they are hopelessly reactionary; they try to go back.

Barclay knew better. He was the progressive, though he expressed himself in terms of seventeenth century theology. He knew that man can no more turn back than time itself can turn back. He knew that man is not a simple animal, but a very complex one, blessed—or cursed—with a sense which distinguishes, though often confusedly, between good and evil, and which proves his salvation or damnation. Once man as a race, or man in childhood as an individual has tasted of the tree of knowledge, he is no longer innocent and irresponsible. His eyes are opened, he looks upon himself, and finds himself naked. He has become self-conscious. And the only way by which he can be free of that self which torments him with its loneliness, its fear of death, its frustrated longings, and its appetites which grow with gratification, is to lose it in the Spirit which is so vastly greater than he. He must yield up his self-will to the divine will. Then, after the self is crucified and buried, will come the resurrection of the soul, a rising of the new man or new creature which Barclay calls the "Christ within."

This is the path taken by the man who chooses the good. For choose he must. Once having partaken of the fruit of knowledge he has no middle ground to stand on. If he merely remains "natural" his course is necessarily evil and he will perish in sin, because sin is a deadness to that Spirit by which alone we may find eternal life.

But Barclay does not speak of nature in its broader aspect as evil. He does not regard animals as evil. He does not consider the natural acts of man's physical being as evil in themselves; when done in the Spirit of God they are useful and answer our end in the creation. Nor does he count man in his infancy as evil, though his racial inheritance as a man has implanted in him both the Seed of Sin and the Seed of Light. With Barclay the term "natural" means sinful only when applied to the man who, after his eyes are opened, is content to remain a mere rational animal indifferent to the light of the Spirit. For him it is sinful to be natural because more is expected of him. Only by pushing forward and through the Spirit may we find communion with God and walk with him again in the cool of the evening.

Nor need one be a nominal Christian or have an outward knowledge of the Scriptures to be so blessed. Where goodness is there is God, for good works are the inevitable fruition of a growing spirit.

Barclay expressed these truths in theological terms because he wrote in an age dominated among the serious minded by theology. It was a theology which seems to the modern mind to have placed more emphasis on man's falling than on Christ's raising him up again. Preachers dwelt at length on infant damnation, and across the seas in Salem men and women were hanged, not for being witches (witchcraft being a recognized form of devil worship) but for the greater sin of refusing to believe that such beings existed. The Quaker faith in man's potential goodness, accepted by us complacently today, was revolutionary heresy to the Puritan clergy of the seventeenth century, and the first section of the *Apology,* dealing with doctrine, is aimed particularly to refute the Calvinistic belief in predestination. This Barclay regarded as a hideous blasphemy against the mercy of God. Accepting Calvin's Seed of Sin Barclay balanced it with a Seed of Light which, if allowed to take root and flourish, would accomplish man's salvation.

But Puritanism, though still a potent force in the life of England at the time the *Apology* was written, had lost its political power in 1660 when Charles II returned from exile. Like his Quaker cousin the king was repelled by the extreme Calvinism of his early Scotch training, but unfortunately his reaction took a less spiritual form. Followed by his court he introduced an era which was as licentious as Puritanism had been grim. Grim though it was Puritanism had had a certain purposefulness, whereas the Restoration was utterly decadent. Its dress was ostentatious, its manners insincere, its morals non-existent. The court of Charles II, aping the French court of Louis XIV, tried to be magnificent and succeeded only in being extravagant, an extravagance for which the people of England had to pay in an increased burden of taxes. Courtiers fawned on the king, addressing him with the plural pronoun "you" while using the common "thou" to inferiors, a pattern passed downward through the social scale.

This was the "Way of the World," to quote the title of a well-known comedy of the period, and it was this worldly way which Barclay protests against in that section of his work devoted to testimonies. Certain of the specific testimonies have grown less significant with changed conditions. Simplicity in dress has become fashionable and in respect to speech every man is now a king, addressed as "you" by all except those of us who cling to the old Quaker way because of its friendly warmth. We can now see plays which, like other forms of art, serve as a medium for truth, and are not of the sort to which Robert Barclay referred when he condemned playgoing.

But if the testimonies are outmoded the spirit behind them is not. We still need to seek simplicity, equality, and the will to peace. Pacifism, of course, is as vital an issue

47

today as it was in the seventeenth century. And in regard to all the testimonies we must keep before us the goal toward which Barclay was working; a way of living whereby we may remain in the world of business and family affection yet maintain a life of the spirit such as is ordinarily possible only in the cloister. This idea, reminiscent of the tertiary orders which were a definite part of medieval monasticism, has found a fuller expression in the writings of Penn.

While in point of doctrine Barclay is refuting Calvinism, and in respect to testimonies protests against the fashionable World, in the middle section of his work, which treats of worship, he challenges both. For the religious sects of his time, whether Roman, Anglican, Puritan, or any of the Nonconformist bodies, however they might vary individually in the amount of ritual or lack of it, were alike in holding religious services dominated by priest or minister. The Society of Friends, on the other hand, sat—and continue to sit—in communal silence, led only by that Spirit from without which works upon the seed within each worshipper.

Many outsiders find this the most outstanding, and to them puzzling, aspect of Quakerism. It is indeed the Society's unique contribution to religion, as Howard Brinton has pointed out in the "Nature of Quakerism," chapter two in his *Quaker Education in Theory and Practice*. From this communal waiting upon the Lord which constitutes the meeting for worship has grown the meeting for business, wherein the temporal affairs of the group are discussed in the light of spiritual guidance. Though Barclay does not mention the business meeting in the *Apology*, he deals with it in his *Anarchy of the Ranters* (published in 1676).

Barclay objected to the more usual forms of worship with their pre-arranged order of service not only because they allowed the human will to dominate instead of the divine will, but also because they imposed a distinction between laity and clergy whereby the worshippers were divided rather than united, and by which religious ministry, which should be open to all was made a trade. This division was infinitely sharper in his day than in ours. He knew a clergy which was corrupt, bigoted, and endued with a passion for theological hair-splitting beyond anything which we can today imagine. To these he refers contemptuously: "Perhaps my method of writing may seem not only different, but even contrary, to that which is commonly used by the men called divines, with which I am not concerned: inasmuch as I confess myself to be not only no imitator and admirer of the schoolmen, but an opposer and despiser of them as such, by whose labour I judge the Christian religion to be so far from being bettered, that it is rather destroyed."

For this reason he despised formal learning. He could afford to, because he had so much of it himself. The *Apology* reveals a knowledge of the Greek philosophers, early church fathers, medieval scholastics, and Protestant reformers which is impressive. Throughout the fourteen propositions which compose the book—treated, incidentally, in the same order as are the propositions in the Westminster Confession—pages are devoted to keen theological argumentation wherein Barclay held his own with highly trained contemporaries. Because this lacks significance today much of it has been omitted, for here we are less interested in what he *did* say than in what he *does* say.

And space is precious for our material is condensed to approximately one tenth of its original wordage. On the whole the space allotted to each major point is proportionate with its treatment in the *Apology*, though more has been

49

given to the peace testimony because of its extreme pertinence in the world of today. Those readers who feel that certain aspects of the subject are presented too meagerly are referred to the *Apology* itself, for which this brief summary is in no way intended as a substitute.

The words are entirely Barclay's own, though cutting has necessarily involved changes in punctuation. They are words which are well worth the reading for their literary style alone, which reflects the vigor and imagery of the mind behind them. For Barclay's approach is fresh and vital, experimental rather than authoritarian, which should endear him to the present age. "What I have heard with the ears of my soul," he tells us, "and seen with my inward eyes, and my hands have handled of the Word of Life, and what hath been inwardly manifested to me of the things of God, that do I declare . . ."

And just how true this is will be discovered by those who read the following pages.

Barclay in Brief

I. BELIEF

SEEING the height of all happiness is placed in the true knowledge of God (*This is life eternal, to know thee the only true God, and Jesus Christ whom thou hast sent*) the true and right understanding of this foundation and ground of knowledge is that which is most necessary to be known and believed in the first place.

Immediate Revelation

We do distinguish betwixt the certain knowledge of God, and the uncertain; betwixt the spiritual knowledge, and the literal; the saving heart-knowledge, and the soaring, airy head-knowledge. The last, we confess, may be divers ways obtained; but the first, by no other way than the inward immediate manifestation and revelation of God's Spirit, shining in and upon the heart, enlightening and opening the understanding.

The certainty of which truth is such, that it hath been acknowledged by some of the most refined and famous of all sorts of professors of Christianity in all ages; who being truly uprighthearted, and earnest seekers of the Lord, (however stated under the disadvantages and epidemical errors of their several sects or ages) the true seed in them hath been answered by God's love, who hath had regard to the good, and hath had of his elect ones among all; who finding a distaste and disgust in all other outward means, even in the very principles and precepts more particularly relative to their own forms and societies, have at last concluded, with one voice, that there was no true knowledge of God, but that which is revealed inwardly by his own Spirit.

The apostle bringeth in the comparison, very apt, and answerable to our purpose and doctrine, that as the things of a man are only known by the spirit of man, so the things of God are only known by the Spirit of God; that is, that as nothing below the spirit of man (as the spirit of brutes, or any other creatures) can properly reach unto or comprehend the things of a man, as being of a nobler and higher nature, so neither can the spirit of man, or the natural man receive nor discern the things of God, or the things that are spiritual, as being also of an higher nature.

Knowledge then of Christ, which is not by the revelation of his own Spirit in the heart, is no more properly the knowledge of Christ, than the prattling of a parrot, which has been taught a few words, may be said to be the voice of a man; for as that, or some other bird, may be taught to sound or utter forth a rational sentence, as it hath learned it by the outward ear, and not from any living principle of reason actuating it; so just such is that knowledge of the things of God, which the natural and carnal man hath gathered from the words or writings of spiritual men.

But as the description of the light of the sun, or of curious colors to a blind man, who, though of the largest capacity, cannot so well understand it by the most acute and lively description, as a child can by seeing them; so neither can the natural man, of the largest capacity, by the best words, even scripture-words, so well understand the mysteries of God's kingdom, as the least and weakest child who tasteth them, by having them revealed inwardly and objectively by the Spirit.

I think it will not be denied, that God's converse with man, all along from Adam to Moses, was by the immediate manifestation of his Spirit: and afterwards, through the whole tract of the law, he spake to his children no otherways; which cannot be denied by such as acknowledge the scriptures of truth to have been written by the inspiration of the Holy Ghost: for these writings, from Moses to Malachi, do declare, that during all that time God revealed himself to his children by his Spirit. And that God revealed himself to his children under the New Testament, to wit, to the apostles, evangelists, and primitive disciples, is confessed by all.

What is proper in this place to be proved is, That Christians now are to be led inwardly and immediately by the Spirit of God, even in the same manner (though it befall not many to be led in the same measure) as the saints were of old.

I shall prove this first from the promise of Christ in these words, John xiv. 16, 17:

And I will pray the Father, and he will give you another Comforter, that he may abide with you forever. Even the Spirit of truth, whom the world cannot receive, because it seeth him not, neither knoweth him; but ye know him, for he dwelleth with you, and shall be in you.

That this Spirit is inward, in my opinion needs no interpretation or commentary. *He dwelleth with you, and shall be in you.* This indwelling of the Spirit in the saints, as it is a thing most needful to be known and believed, so is it as positively asserted in the scripture as anything else can be.

He then that acknowledges himself ignorant and a stranger to the inward in-being of the Spirit of Christ in his heart, doth thereby acknowledge himself to be yet in the carnal mind, which is enmity to God; and in short, whatever he may otherwise know or believe of Christ, or however much skilled or acquainted with the letter of the holy scripture, not yet to be, notwithstanding all that, attained to the least degree of a Christian; yea, not once to have embraced the Christian religion. For take but away the Spirit, and Christianity remains no more than the dead carcase of a man, when the soul and spirit is departed, remains a man; which the living can no more abide, but do bury out of their sight, as a noisome and useless thing, however acceptable it hath been when actuated and moved by the soul. Lastly, whatsoever is excellent, whatsoever is noble, whatsoever is worthy, whatsoever is desirable in the Christian faith, is ascribed to this Spirit, without which it could no more subsist than the outward world without the sun. Hereunto have all true Christians, in all ages, attributed their strength and life.

And what shall I say more? For the time would fail me to tell of all those things which the holy men of old have declared, and the saints of this day do themselves enjoy, by the virtue and power of this Spirit dwelling in them. If therefore it be so, why should any be so foolish as to deny, or so unwise as not to seek after this Spirit, which Christ hath promised shall dwell in his children? They then that do suppose the indwelling and leading of his Spirit to be ceased, must also suppose Christianity to be ceased which cannot subsist without it.

Seeing then that Christ hath promised his Spirit to lead his children, and that every one of them both ought and may be led by it, if any depart from this certain guide in deeds, and yet in words pretend to be led by it, into things that are not good, it will not from thence follow, that the true guidance of the Spirit is uncertain, or ought not to be followed; no more than it will follow that the sun sheweth not light, because a blind man or one who wilfully shuts his eyes, falls into a ditch at noon-day for want of light; or that no words are spoken, because a deaf man hears them not; or that a garden full of fragrant flowers has no sweet smell, because he that has lost his smelling doth not smell it.

All these mistakes therefore are to be ascribed to the weakness or wickedness of men, and not to that Holy Spirit.

Moreover, these divine inward revelations, which we make absolutely necessary for the building up of true faith, neither do nor can ever contradict the outward testimony of the scriptures, or right and sound reason. Yet from hence it will not follow, that these divine revelations are to be subjected to the test, either of the outward testimony of the scriptures, or of the natural reason of man, as to a more noble or certain rule and touchstone; for this divine revelation, and inward illumination, is that which is evident and clear of itself, forcing, by its own evidence and clearness, the well-disposed understanding to assent.

The Scriptures

From these revelations of the Spirit of God to the saints have proceeded the Scriptures of Truth.

Because they are only a declaration of the fountain, and not the fountain itself, therefore they are not to be esteemed the principal ground of all truth and knowledge, nor yet the adequate primary rule of faith and manners. Yet because they give a true and faithful testimony of the first foundation, they are and may be esteemed a secondary rule, subordinate to the Spirit, from which they have all their excellency and certainty; for as by the inward testimony of the Spirit we do alone truly know them, so they testify, that the Spirit is that Guide by which the saints are led into all Truth; therefore, according to the scriptures, the Spirit is the first and principal leader.

Through and by the clearness which that Spirit gives us it is that we are only best rid of those difficulties that occur to us concerning the scriptures. The real and undoubted experience whereof I myself have been a witness of, with great admiration of the love of God to his children in these latter days: for I have known some of my friends, who profess the same faith with me, faithful servants of the Most High God, and full of divine knowledge of his truth, as it was immediately and inwardly revealed to them by the spirit, from a true and living experience, who not only were ignorant of the Greek and Hebrew, but even some of them could not read their own language, who being pressed by their adversaries with some citations out of the English translation, and finding them to disagree with the manifestation of truth in their own hearts, have boldly affirmed the Spirit of God never said so, and that it was certainly wrong; for they did not believe that any of the holy prophets or apostles had ever written so; which when I on this account seriously examined, I really found to be errors and corruptions of the translators; who (as in most translations) do not so much give us the genuine signification of the words, as strain them to express that which comes nearest to that opinion and notion they have of truth.

If it be then asked me, Whether I think hereby to render the scriptures altogether uncertain, or useless?

I answer; Not at all, provided that to the Spirit from which they came be but granted that place the scriptures themselves give it, I do freely concede to the scriptures the second place.

For tho' God doth principally and chiefly lead us by his

Spirit, yet he sometimes conveys his comfort and consolation to us through his children, whom he raises up and inspires to speak or write a word in season, whereby the saints are made instruments in the hand of the Lord to strengthen and encourage one another, which doth also tend to perfect and make them wise unto salvation; and such as are led by the Spirit cannot neglect, but do naturally love, and are wonderfully cherished by, that which proceedeth from the same Spirit in another; because such mutual emanations of the heavenly life tend to quicken the mind, when at any time it is overtaken with heaviness.

Secondly, God hath seen meet that herein we should, as in a looking glass, see the conditions and experiences of the saints of old; that finding our experience answer to theirs, we might thereby be the more confirmed and comforted, and our hope of obtaining the same end strengthened; that observing the providences attending them, seeing the snares they were liable to, and beholding their deliverances, we may thereby be made wise unto salvation, and seasonably reproved and instructed in righteousness.

This is the great work of the scriptures, and their service to us, that we may witness them fulfilled in us, and so discern the stamp of God's Spirit and ways upon them, by the inward acquaintance we have with the same Spirit and work in our hearts.

The Condition of Man in the Fall

Hitherto we have discoursed how the true knowledge of God is attained and served; also of what use and service the holy scripture is to the saints. We come now to examine the state and condition of man as he stands in the fall; what his capacity and power is; and how far he is able, as of himself, to advance in relation to the things of God.

We confess that a seed of sin is transmitted to all men from Adam, although imputed to none, until by sinning they actually join with it; in which seed he gave occasion to all to sin, and it is the origin of all evil actions and thoughts in men's hearts, as it is in Rom. v. i.e. *In which death all have sinned.* For this seed of sin is frequently called death in the scripture, and the body of death; seeing indeed it is a death to the life of righteousness and holiness: therefore its seed and its product is called the old man, the old Adam, in which all sin is; for which we use this name to express this sin, and not that of original sin; of which phrase the scripture makes no mention, and under which invented and unscriptural barbarism this notion of imputed sin to infants took place among Christians.

Many of the heathen philosophers were sensible of the loss received by Adam, though they knew not the outward history: hence Plato asserted, That man's soul was fallen into a dark cave, where it only conversed with shadows. Pythagoras saith, Man wandereth in this world as a stranger, banished from the presence of God. And Plotinus compareth man's soul, fallen from God, to a cinder, or dead coal, out of which the fire is extinguished. Some of them said, That the wings of the soul were clipped or fallen off, so that they could not flee unto God. All which, and many more such expressions, that might be gathered out of their writings, shew that they were not without a sense of this loss.

The consequence of this fall is also expressed, Gen. iii. 24. *So he drove out the man, and he placed at the east of the garden of Eden cherubims, and a flaming sword, which turned every way, to keep the way of the tree of life.* Now whatsoever literal signification this may have, we may safely ascribe to this paradise a mystical signification, and truly account it that spiritual communion and fellowship, which the saints obtain with God by Jesus Christ; to whom only these cherubims give way, and unto as many as enter by him, who calls himself the Door. For whatsoever real good any man doth, it proceedeth not from his nature, as he is a man, or the son of Adam; but from the seed of God in him, as a new visitation of life.

Universal and Saving Light

We have considered man's fallen, lost, corrupted, and degenerated condition. Now it is fit to enquire, how and by what means he may come to be freed out of this miserable and depraved condition.

As the knowledge thereof has been manifested to us by the revelation of Jesus Christ in us, fortified by our own sensible experience, and sealed by the testimony of the Spirit in our hearts, we can confidently affirm, and clearly evince, according to the testimony of the holy scriptures that: GOD, out of his infinite love, who delighteth not in the death of a sinner, but that all should live and be saved, hath *so loved the world, that he hath given his only Son a* LIGHT, *that whosoever believeth in him shall be saved,* John iii. 16. *who enlighteneth EVERY man that cometh into the world,* John i. 9. *and maketh manifest all things that are reprovable,* Ephes. v. 13. and teacheth all temperance, righteousness, and godliness; and this Light enlighteneth the hearts of all for a time, in order to salvation; and this is it which reproves the sin of all individuals, and would work out the salvation of all, if not resisted. Nor is it less universal than the seed of sin, being the purchase of his death, who tasted death for every man: *for as in Adam all die, even so in Christ all shall be made alive,* I Cor. xv. 22.

According to which principle or hypothesis all the objections against the universality of Christ's death are easily solved; neither is it needful to recur to the ministry of angels, and those other miraculous means which they say God useth to manifest the doctrine and history of Christ's passion unto such, who, living in parts of the world where the outward preaching of the gospel is unknown, have well improved the first and common grace.

Hence Justin Martyr stuck not to call Socrates a Christian, saying that all such as lived according to the divine word in them, which was in all men, were Christians, such as Socrates and Heraclitus, and others among the Greeks.

For as hence it well follows that some of the old philosophers might have been saved, so also may some, who by providence are cast into those remote parts of the world where the knowledge of the history is wanting, be made partakers of the divine mystery, if they suffer his seed and light, enlightening their hearts, to take place, in which light communion with the Father and the Son is enjoyed, so as of wicked men to become holy, and lovers of that power, by whose inward and secret touches they feel themselves turned from the evil to the good, and learn to do to others as they would be done by, in which Christ himself affirms all to be included.

This is that Christ within, which we are heard so much to speak and declare of, everywhere preaching him up, and exhorting people to believe in the light, and obey it, that they may come to know Christ in them, to deliver them from all sin.

We have said how that a divine, spiritual, and supernatural light is in all men; also how that, as it is received and closed within the heart, Christ comes to be formed and brought forth: but we are far from ever having said, that

Christ is thus formed in all men, or in the wicked: for that is a great attainment, which the apostle travailed that it might be brought forth in the Galatians. Neither is Christ in all men by way of union, or indeed, to speak strictly, by way of inhabitation; because this inhabitation, as it is generally taken, imports union, or the manner of Christ's being in the saints. But in regard Christ is in all men as in a seed, yea, and that he never is nor can be separate from that holy pure seed and light which is in all men; in this respect then, as he is in the seed which is in all men, we have said Christ is in all men, and have preached and directed all men to Christ in them, who lies crucified in them by their sins and iniquities, that they may look upon him whom they have pierced, and repent: whereby he that now lies as it were slain and buried in them, may come to be raised, and have dominion in their hearts over all.

Though then this seed be small in its appearance, so that Christ compares it to *a grain of mustard-seed, which is the least of all seeds*, Matth. xiii. 31, 32. and that it be hid in the earthly part of man's heart; yet therein is life and salvation towards the sons of men wrapped up, which comes to be revealed as they give way to it. And this seed in the hearts of all men is the kingdom of God, as in capacity to be produced, or rather exhibited, according as it receives depth, is nourished, and not choaked. And as the whole body of a great tree is wrapped up potentially in the seed of the tree, and so is brought forth in due season, even so the kingdom of Jesus Christ, yea Jesus Christ himself, Christ within, who is the hope of glory, and becometh wisdom, righteousness, sanctification and redemption, is in every man's and woman's heart, in that little incorruptible seed, ready to be brought forth.

This leads me to speak concerning the manner of this

seed or light's operation in the hearts of all men. To them then that ask us after this manner, If two men have equal sufficient light and grace, and the one be saved by it, the other not? is not then the will of man the cause of the one's salvation beyond the other?

I say, to such we thus answer: That as the grace and light in all is sufficient to save all, and of its own nature would save all; so it strives and wrestles with all in order to save them; he that resists its striving, is the cause of his own condemnation; he that resists it not, it becomes his salvation: for that in him that is saved, the working is of the grace, and not of the man; and it is a passiveness rather than an act; though afterwards, as man is wrought upon, there is a will raised in him, by which he comes to be a co-worker with the grace: for according to that of Augustine, He that made us without us, will not save us without us. So that the first step is not by man's working, but by his not contrary working. And we believe, that at these singular seasons of every man's visitation, as man is wholly unable of himself to work with the grace, neither can he move one step out of the natural condition, until the grace lay hold upon him; so it is possible for him to be passive, and not to resist it, as it is possible for him to resist it. So we say, the grace of God works in and upon man's nature; which, though of itself wholly corrupted and defiled, and prone to evil, yet is capable to be wrought upon by the grace of God; even as iron, though an hard and cold metal of itself, may be warmed and softened by the heat of the fire, and wax melted by the sun. And as iron or wax, when removed from the fire or sun, returneth to its former condition of cold-ness and hardness; so man's heart, as it resist or retires from the grace of God, returns to its former condition again.

62

Reason

It will manifestly appear by what is above said, that we understand not this divine principle to be any part of man's nature, nor yet to be any reliques of any good which Adam lost by his fall. For we certainly know that this light of which we speak is not only distinct but of a different nature from the soul of man, and its faculties. Indeed that man, as he is a rational creature, hath reason as a natural faculty of his soul, by which he can discern things that are rational, we deny not; for this is a property natural and essential to him, by which he can know and learn many arts and sciences, beyond what any other animal can do by the mere animal principle. Neither do we deny but by this rational principle man may apprehend in his brain, and in the notion, a knowledge of God and spiritual things; yet that not being the right organ, it cannot profit him towards salvation, but rather hindereth; and indeed the great cause of the apostasy hath been, that man hath sought to fathom the things of God in and by this natural and rational principle, and to build up a religion in it, neglecting and overlooking this principle and seed of God in the heart; so that herein, in the most universal and catholick sense, hath Anti-Christ in every man set up himself, and sitteth in the temple of God as God, and above every thing that is called God. For men *being the temple of the Holy Ghost,* as saith the apostle, I Cor. iii. 16. when the rational principle sets up itself there above the seed of God, to reign and rule as a prince in spiritual things, while the holy seed is wounded and bruised, there is Anti-Christ in every man, or somewhat exalted above and against Christ.

Nevertheless we do not hereby affirm as if man had received his reason to no purpose, or to be of no service unto

63

him, in no wise; we look upon reason as fit to order and rule man in things natural. For as God gave two great Lights to rule the outward world, the sun and moon, the greater light to rule the day, and the lesser light to rule the night; so hath he given man the light of his Son, a spiritual divine light, to rule him in things spiritual, and the light of reason to rule him in things natural. And even as the moon borrows her light from the sun, so ought men, if they would be rightly and comfortably ordered in natural things, to have their reason enlightened by this divine and pure light. Which enlightened reason, in those that obey and follow this true light, we confess may be useful to man even in spiritual things, as even as the animal life in man, regulated and ordered by his reason, helps him in going about things that are rational.

Conscience

We do further rightly distinguish this from man's natural conscience; for conscience being that in man which ariseth from the natural faculties of man's soul, may be defiled and corrupted.

Now conscience, to define it truly, comes from *conscire*, and is that knowledge which ariseth in man's heart, from what agreeth, contradicteth, or is contrary to any thing believed by him, whereby he becomes conscious to himself that he transgresseth by doing that which he is persuaded he ought not to do. So that the mind being once blinded or defiled with a wrong belief, there ariseth a conscience from that belief, which troubles him when he goes against it. As for example; A Turk who hath possessed himself with a false belief that it is unlawful for him to drink wine, if he do it, his conscience smites him for it; but though he keep

64

many concubines, his conscience troubles him not, because his judgment is already defiled with a false opinion that it is lawful for him to do the one, and unlawful to do the other.

For conscience followeth judgment, doth not inform it; but this light, as it is received, removes the blindness of the judgment, opens the understanding, and rectifies both the judgment and conscience. So we confess also, that conscience is an excellent thing, where it is rightly informed and enlightened: wherefore some of us have fitly compared it to the lanthorn, and the light of Christ to a candle; a lanthorn is useful when a clear candle burns and shines in it: but otherwise of no use. To the light of Christ then in the conscience, and not to man's natural conscience, it is that we continually commend men.

Justification by Faith and Works*

As many as resist not this light, but receive the same, it becomes in them an holy, pure, and spiritual birth; by which holy birth, to wit, Jesus Christ formed within us, and working his works in us, as we are sanctified, so are we justified in the sight of God.

Since good works as naturally follow from this birth as heat from fire, therefore are they of absolute necessity to justification. Wherefore their judgment is false and against the truth that say, that the holiest works of the saints are defiled and sinful in the sight of God: for these good works are not the works of the law, excluded by the apostle from justification.

I say, there is a great difference betwixt the works of the

---

* In this section Barclay rejects the then commonly accepted Protestant doctrine that man is justified or accounted righteous by the sacrifice of Christ, accepted by faith, regardless of whether or not he is actually righteous.

law, and those of grace, or of the gospel. The first are excluded, the second not, but are necessary. The first are those which are performed in man's own will, and by his strength, in a conformity to the outward law and letter; and therefore are man's own imperfect works, or works of the law, which makes nothing perfect: and to this belong all the ceremonies, purifications, washings, and traditions of the Jews. The second are the works of the Spirit of grace in the heart, wrought in conformity to the inward and spiritual law; which works are not wrought in man's will, nor by his power and ability, but in and by the power and Spirit of Christ in us, and therefore are pure and perfect in their kind (as shall hereafter be proved) and may be called Christ's works, for that he is the immediate author and worker of them: such works we affirm absolutely necessary to justification, so that a man cannot be justified without them; and all faith without them is dead and useless, as the apostle James saith. But faith, which worketh by love, is that which availeth, which is absolutely necessary: for faith, that worketh by love, cannot be without works.

Perfection

Since we have placed justification in the revelation of Jesus Christ formed and brought forth in the heart, there working his works of righteousness, and bringing forth the fruits of the Spirit, the question is, How far he may prevail in us while we are in this life, or we over our souls' enemies, in and by his strength?

We do believe, that to those in whom this pure and holy birth is fully brought forth, the body of death and sin comes to be crucified and removed, and their hearts united and subjected to the truth; so as not to obey any suggestions or temptations of the evil one, but to be free from actual sinning and transgressing of the law of God, and in that respect perfect.

By this we understand not such a perfection as may not daily admit of growth, and consequently mean not as if we were to be as pure, holy, and perfect as God in his divine attributes of wisdom, knowledge, and purity; but only a perfection proportionable and answerable to man's measure, whereby we are kept from transgressing the law of God, and enabled to answer what he requires of us; even as he that improved his two talents so as to make four of them, perfected his work, and was so accepted of his Lord as to be called a good and faithful servant, nothing less than he that made his five ten.

Though a man may witness this for a season, and therefore all ought to press after it; yet we do not affirm but those that have attained it in a measure may, by the wiles and temptations of the enemy, fall into iniquity, and lose it sometimes, if they be not watchful, and do not diligently attend to that of God in the heart. And we doubt not but many good and holy men, who have arrived to everlasting life, have had divers ebbings and flowings of this kind; for though every sin weakens a man in his spiritual condition, yet it doth not so as to destroy him altogether, or render him uncapable of rising again.

Nevertheless, I will not affirm that a state is not attainable in this life, in which to do righteousness may be so natural to the regenerate soul, that in the stability of that condition he cannot sin.

So then, if thou desirest to know this perfection and freedom from sin possible for thee, turn thy mind to the light and spiritual law of Christ in the heart, and suffer the reproofs thereof; so that that life that sometimes was alive in thee to this world, and the love and lusts thereof, may die, and a new life be raised, by which thou mayest live henceforward to God, and not to or for thyself; and with the apostle thou mayest say, Gal. ii. 20. *It is no more I, but Christ alive in me:* And then thou wilt be a Christian indeed.

II. WORSHIP

The Church

HITHERTO I have treated of those things, which relate to the Christian faith and Christians, as they stand each in his private and particular condition, and how and by what means every man may be a Christian indeed and so abide. Now I come in order to speak of those things that relate to Christians, as they are stated in a joint fellowship and communion, and come under a visible and outward society, which society is called the church of God, and in scripture compared to a body, and therefore named the body of Christ.

The Church then, according to the grammatical signification of the word, as it is used in the holy scripture, signifies an assembly or gathering of many into one place; and indeed, as this is the grammatical sense of the word, so also it is the real and proper signification of the thing, the church being no other thing but the society, gathering, or company of such as God hath called out of the world, and worldly spirit, to walk in his LIGHT and LIFE. The church then so defined is to be considered, as it comprehends all that are thus called and gathered truly by God, both such as are yet in this inferior world, and such as having already laid down the earthly tabernacle, are passed into their heavenly mansions, which together do make up the one catholick church, concerning which there is so much controversy. Out of which church we freely acknowledge there can be no salvation; because under this church and its denomination are comprehended all, and as many, of whatsoever nation, kindred, tongue, or people they be, though

69

outwardly strangers, and remote from those who profess Christ and Christianity in words, and have the benefit of the scriptures, as become obedient to the holy light and testimony of God in their hearts, so as to become sanctified by it, and cleansed from the evils of their ways. There may be members therefore of this catholick church both among heathens, Turks, Jews, and all the several sorts of Christians, men and women of integrity and simplicity of heart, who though blinded in some things in their understanding, and perhaps burdened with the superstitions and formality of the several sects in which they are ingrossed, yet being upright in their hearts before the Lord, chiefly aiming and labouring to be delivered from iniquity, and loving to follow righteousness, are by the secret touches of this holy light in their souls enlivened and quickened, thereby secretly united to God, and therethrough become true members of this catholick church.

Group Worship

All true and acceptable worship to God is offered in the inward and immediate moving and drawing of his own Spirit, which is neither limited to places, time, nor persons. For tho' we are to worship him always, and continually to fear before him; yet as to the outward signification thereof, in prayers, praises or preachings, we ought not to do it in our own will, where and when we will; but where and when we are moved thereunto by the stirring and secret inspiration of the Spirit of God in our hearts; which God heareth and accepteth of, and is never wanting to move us thereunto, when need is; of which he himself is the alone proper judge. All other worship then, both praises, prayers, or preachings, which man sets about in his own will, and at his own appointment, which he can both begin and end at his pleasure, do or leave undone as himself seeth meet, whether they be a prescribed form, as a liturgy, &c. or prayers conceived extempore by the natural strength and faculty of the mind, they are all but superstition, will-worship, and abominable idolatry in the sight of God, which are now to be denied and rejected, and separated from, in this day of his spiritual arising.

Yet I would not be understood, as if I intended the putting away of all set times and places to worship: God forbid I should think of such an opinion. Nay, we are none of those that forsake the assembling of ourselves together; but have even certain times and places, in which we carefully meet together (nor can we be driven therefrom by the threats and persecutions of men) to wait upon God, and worship him. To meet together we think necessary for the people of God; because, so long as we are cloathed with this outward tabernacle, there is a necessity to the entertaining of a joint and visible fellowship, and bearing of an outward testimony for God, and seeing of the faces of one another, that we concur with our persons as well as spirits: to be accompanied with that inward love and unity of spirit doth greatly tend to encourage and refresh the saints.

And as every one is thus gathered, and so met together inwardly in their spirits, as well as outwardly in their persons, there the secret power and virtue of life is known to refresh the soul, and the pure motions and breathings of God's Spirit are felt to arise; from which, as words of declaration, prayers or praises arise, the acceptable worship is known, which edifies the church, and is well-pleasing to God. And no man here limits the Spirit of God, nor bringeth forth his own conned and gathered stuff; but every one puts that forth which the Lord puts into their hearts: and it is uttered forth not in man's will and wisdom, but in the evi-

71

dence and demonstration of the Spirit, and of power. Yea, though there be not a word spoken, yet is the true spiritual worship performed, and the body of Christ edified; yea, it may, and hath often fallen out among us, that divers meetings have passed without one word; and yet our souls have been greatly edified and refreshed, and our hearts wonderfully overcome with the secret sense of God's power and Spirit, which without words hath been ministered from one vessel to another.

Yea, sometimes, when there is not a word in the meeting, but all are silently waiting, if one come in that is rude and wicked, and in whom the power of darkness prevaileth much, perhaps with an intention to mock or do mischief, if the whole meeting be gathered into the life, and it be raised in a good measure, it will strike terror into such an one, and he will feel himself unable to resist; but by the secret strength and virtue thereof, the power of darkness in him will be chained down: and if the day of his visitation be not expired, it will reach to the measure of grace in him, and raise it up to the redeeming of his soul. For not a few have come to be convinced of the truth after this manner, of which I myself, in part, am a true witness, who not by strength of arguments, or by a particular disquisition of each doctrine, and convincement of my understanding thereby, came to receive and bear witness of the truth, but by being secretly reached by this life; for when I came into the silent assemblies of God's people, I felt a secret power among them, which touched my heart, and as I gave way unto it, I found the evil weakening in me, and the good raised up, and so I became thus knit and united unto them, hungering more and more after the increase of this power and life, whereby I might feel myself perfectly redeemed.

Many are the blessed experiences which I could relate of

this silence and manner of worship; yet I do not so much commend and speak of silence as if we had bound ourselves by any law to exclude praying or preaching, or tied ourselves thereunto, not at all: for as our worship consisteth not in words, so neither in silence, as silence; but in an holy dependence of the mind upon God: from which dependence silence necessarily follows in the first place, until words can be brought forth, which are from God's Spirit.

And God is not wanting to move in his children to bring forth words of exhortation and prayer, when it is needful; so that of the many gatherings and meetings of such as are convinced of the truth, there is scarce any in whom God raiseth not up some or other to minister to his brethren; and there are few meetings that are altogether silent. For when many are met together in this one life and name, it doth most naturally and frequently excite them to pray to and praise God, and stir up one another by mutual exhortation and instructions: yet we judge it needful there be in the first place some time of silence, during which every one may be gathered inward to the word and gift of grace, from which he that ministereth may receive strength to bring forth what he ministereth.

This great duty then of waiting upon God, must needs be exercised in man's denying self, both inwardly and outwardly, in a still and mere dependence upon God, in abstracting from all the workings, imaginations, and speculations of his own mind, that being emptied as it were of himself, and so thoroughly crucified to the natural products thereof, he may be fit to receive the Lord, who will have no co-partner nor co-rival of his glory and power. And man being thus stated, the little seed of righteousness which God hath planted in his soul, and Christ hath purchased for him, even the measure of grace and life, which is burdened and crucified by man's natural thoughts and imaginations, receives a place to arise, and becometh a holy birth and geniture in man; and is that divine air in and by which man's soul and spirit comes to be leavened; and by waiting therein he comes to be accepted in the sight of God, to stand in his presence, hear his voice, and observe the motions of his holy Spirit.

As iron sharpeneth iron, the seeing of the faces one of another, when both are inwardly gathered unto the life, giveth occasion for the life secretly to rise, and pass from vessel to vessel. And as many candles lighted, and put in one place, do greatly augment the light, and make it more to shine forth, so when many are gathered together into the same life, there is more of the glory of God, and his power appears, to the refreshment of each individual; for that he partakes not only of the light and life raised in himself, but in all the rest.

And therefore the Lord oftentimes, when any turn towards him, and have true desires thus to wait upon him, and find great difficulty through the unstayedness of their minds, doth in condescension and compassion cause his power to break forth in a more strong and powerful manner. And when the mind sinks down, and waits for the appearance of life, and that the power of darkness in the soul wrestles and works against it, then the good seed, as it ariseth, will be found to work as physick in the soul, especially if such a weak one be in the assembly of divers others in whom the life is arisen in greater dominion, and through the contrary workings of the power of darkness there will be found an inward striving in the soul as really in the mystery as ever Esau and Jacob strove in Rebecca's womb. And from this inward travail, while the darkness seeks to obscure the light, and the light breaks through the darkness,

which it always will do, if the soul gives not its strength
to the darkness, there will be such a painful travail found
in the soul, that will even work upon the outward man, so
that oftentimes, through the working thereof, the body will
be greatly shaken, and many groans, and sighs, and tears,
even as the pangs of a woman in travail, will lay hold upon
it; yea, and this not only as to one, but when the enemy,
who when the children of God assemble together is not
wanting to be present, hath prevailed in any measure in a
whole meeting, and strongly worketh against it by spread-
ing and propagating his dark power, and by drawing out
the minds of such as are met from the life in them, as they
come to be sensible of this power of his that works against
them, and to wrestle with it by the armour of light, sometimes the power of God will break forth into a whole meeting, and there will be such an inward travail, while each is
seeking to overcome the evil in themselves, that by the
strong contrary workings of these opposite powers, like the
going of two contrary tides, every individual will be
strongly exercised as in a day of battle, and thereby trembling and a motion of body will be upon most, if not upon
all, which, as the power of truth prevails, will from pangs
and groans end with a sweet sound of thanksgiving and
praise. And from this the name of Quakers, i. e. Tremblers,
was first reproachfully cast upon us; which though it be
none of our choosing, yet in this respect we are not ashamed
of it, but have rather reason to rejoice therefore, even that
we are sensible of this power that hath oftentimes laid hold
of our adversaries, and made them yield unto us, and join
with us, and confess to the truth, before they had any distinct or discursive knowledge of our doctrines, so that
sometimes many at one meeting have been thus convinced:
and this power would sometimes also reach to and wonder-

75

fully work even in little children, to the admiration and astonishment of many.

The great advantage of this true worship of God, which we profess and practise, is, that it consisteth not in man's wisdom, riches nor splendor of this world to beautify it, as being of a spiritual and heavenly nature; and therefore too simple and contemptible to the natural mind and will of man, that hath no delight to abide in it, because he finds no room there for his imagination and inventions, and hath not the opportunity to gratify his outward and carnal senses: so that this form being observed, is not likely to be long kept pure without the power; for it is of itself so naked without it, that it hath nothing in it to invite and tempt men to dote upon it, further than it is accompanied with the power.

Ministry

And when they assemble together to wait upon God, and to worship and adore him; then such as the Spirit sets apart for the ministry, by its divine power and influence opening their mouths, and giving them to exhort, reprove, and instruct with virtue and power; these are thus ordained of God and admitted into the ministry, and their brethren cannot but hear them, receive them, and also honour them for their work's sake. And so this is not monopolized by a certain kind of men, as the clergy (who are to that purpose educated and brought up as other carnal artists) and the rest to be despised as laicks; but it is left to the free gift of God to choose any whom he seeth meet thereunto, whether rich or poor, servant or master, young or old, yea, male or female.

As by the light or gift of God all true knowledge in things spiritual is received and revealed, so by the same, as it is manifested and received in the heart, by the strength and power thereof, every true minister of the gospel is ordained, prepared, and supplied in the work of the ministry; and by the leading, moving, and drawing hereof ought every evangelist and Christian pastor to be led and ordered in his labour and work of the gospel, both as to the place where, as to the persons to whom, and as to the time wherein he is to minister. Moreover they who have this authority may and ought to preach the gospel, though without human commission or literature; as on the other hand, they who want the authority of this divine gift, however learned, or authorized by the commission of men and churches, are to be esteemed but as deceivers, and not true ministers of the gospel. Also they who have received this holy and unspotted gift, as they have freely received it, so are they freely to give it, without hire or bargaining, far less to use it as a Trade to get money by.

Of a liberty to speak or prophesy by the Spirit, I say all may do that, when moved thereunto, as above is shewn; but we do believe and affirm that some are more particularly called to the work of the ministry, and therefore are fitted of the Lord for that purpose; whose work is more constantly and particularly to instruct, exhort, admonish, oversee, and watch over their brethren; and that as there is something more incumbent upon them in that respect than upon every common believer, so also, as in that relation, there is due to them from the flock such obedience and subjection as is mentioned in these testimonies of the scripture, Heb. xiii. 17. I Thess. v. 12, 13. I Tim. v. 17. I Pet. v. 5. Also besides these who are thus particularly called to the ministry, and constant labor in the work and doctrine, there are also the elders, who though they be not moved to a frequent testimony by way of declaration in words, yet as such are grown up on the experience of the blessed work of truth in their hearts, they watch over and privately admonish the young, take care for the widows, the poor, and fatherless, and look that nothing be wanting, but that peace, love, unity, concord, and soundness be preserved in the church of Christ; and this answers to the deacons mentioned Acts vi.

That which we oppose, is the distinction of laity and clergy, which in the scripture is not to be found, whereby none are admitted unto the work of the ministry but such as are educated at schools on purpose, and instructed in logick and philosophy, &c. and so are at their apprenticeship to learn the art and trade of preaching, even as a man learns any other art, whereby all other honest mechanick men, who have not got this heathenish art, are excluded from having this privilege. And so he that is a scholar thus bred up must not have any honest trade whereby to get him a livelihood, if he once intend for the ministry, but he must see to get him a place, and then he hath his set hire for a livelihood to him. He must also be distinguished from the rest by the colour of his cloaths; for he must only wear black, and must be a master of arts.

The ministers we plead for, are such as having freely received, freely give; who covet no man's silver, gold, or garments; who seek no man's goods, but seek them, and the salvation of their souls: whose hands supply their own necessities, working honestly for bread to themselves and their families. And if at any time they be called of God, so as the work of the Lord hinder them from the use of their trades, take what is freely given them by such to whom they have communicated spirituals; and having food and raiment, are therewith content.

For in our day, God hath raised up witnesses for himself,

as he did fishermen of old; many, yea, most of whom, are labouring and mechanick men, who, altogether without that learning, have, by the power and Spirit of God, struck at the very root and ground of Babylon; and in the strength and might of this power, have gathered thousands, by reaching their consciences, into the same power and life, who, as to the outward part, have been far more knowing than they, yet not able to resist the virtue that proceeded from them. Of which I myself am a true witness; and can declare from certain experience, because my heart hath been often greatly broken and tendered by that virtuous life that proceeded from the powerful ministry of those illiterate men: so that by their very countenance, as well as words, I have felt the evil in me often chained down, and the good reached to and raised. What shall I then say to you, who are lovers of learning, and admirers of knowledge? Was not I also a lover and admirer of it, who also sought after it, according to my age and capacity? But it pleased God, in his unutterable love, early to withstand my vain endeavours, while I was yet but eighteen years of age; and made me seriously to consider (which I wish also may befall others) that without holiness and regeneration, no man can see God. If ye consider these things, then will ye say with me, that all this learning, wisdom and knowledge, gathered in this fallen nature, is but as dross and dung, in comparison of the cross of Christ; especially being destitute of that power, life and virtue, which I perceived these excellent (though despised, because illiterate) witnesses of God to be filled with: and therefore seeing, that in and among them, I, with many others, have found the heavenly food that gives contentment, let my soul seek after this learning, and wait for it forever.

Prayer

Having hitherto spoken of preaching, now it is fit to speak of praying, concerning which the like controversy ariseth. Our adversaries, whose religion is all for the most part outside, and such whose acts are the mere product of man's natural will and abilities, as they can preach, so can they pray when they please, and therefore have their set particular prayers. I meddle not with the controversies among themselves concerning this, some of them being for set prayers, as a liturgy, others for such as are conceived extempore: it suffices me that all of them agree in this, That the motions and influence of the Spirit of God are not necessary to be previous thereunto; and therefore they have set times in their publick worship, as before and after preaching, and in their private devotion, as morning and evening, and before and after meat, and other such occasions, at which they precisely set about the performing of their prayers, by speaking words to God, whether they feel any motion or influence of the Spirit or not.

We freely confess that prayer is both very profitable, and a necessary duty commanded, and fit to be practised frequently by all Christians; but as we can do nothing without Christ, so neither can we pray without the concurrence and assistance of his Spirit. But that the state of the controversy may be the better understood, let it be considered, first, that prayer is two-fold, inward and outward. Inward prayer is that secret turning of the mind towards God, whereby, being secretly touched and awakened by the light of Christ in the conscience, and so bowed down under the sense of its iniquities, unworthiness, and misery, it looks up to God, and joining with the secret shining of the seed of God, it breathes towards him, and is constantly breathing forth some secret desires and aspirations towards him. It is in this sense that we are so frequently in scripture commanded to pray continually, Luke xviii. 1. I Thess. v. 17. Eph. vi. 18. Luke xxi. 36. which cannot be understood of outward prayer, because it was impossible that men should be always upon their knees, expressing words of prayer; and this would hinder them from the exercise of those duties no less positively commanded. Outward prayer is, when as the spirit, being thus in the exercise of inward retirement, and feeling the breathing of the Spirit of God to arise powerfully in the soul, receives strength and liberty by a super-added motion and influence of the Spirit to bring forth either audible sighs, groans, or words, and that either in public assemblies, or in private, or at meat, &c.

Therefore such as are diligent and watchful in their minds, and much retired in the exercise of this inward prayer, are more capable to be frequent in the use of the outward, because that this holy influence doth more constantly attend them, and they being better acquainted with, and accustomed to, the motions of God's Spirit, can easily perceive and discern them. And indeed, as such who are most diligent have a near access to God, and he taketh most delight to draw them by his Spirit to approach and call upon him, so when many are gathered together in this watchful mind, God doth frequently pour forth the Spirit of prayer among them and stir them thereunto, to the edifying and building up of one another in love. But because this outward prayer depends upon the inward, as that which must follow it, and cannot be acceptably performed but as attended with a superadded influence and motion of the Spirit, therefore cannot we prefix set times to pray outwardly, so as to lay a necessity to speak words at such and such times, whether we feel this heavenly influence and assistance or no; for that we judge were a tempting of

81

God, and a coming before him without due preparation.

Song

As to the singing of psalms, there will not be need of any long discourse; for that the case is just the same as in the two former of preaching and prayer. We confess this to be a part of God's worship, and very sweet and refreshing, when it proceeds from a true sense of God's love in the heart, and arises from the divine influence of the Spirit, which leads souls to breathe forth either a sweet harmony, or words suitable to the present condition; whether they be words formerly used by the saints, and recorded in scripture, such as the Psalms of David, or other words.

That singing then that pleaseth him must proceed from that which is pure in the heart (even from the Word of Life therein) in and by which, richly dwelling in us, spiritual songs and hymns are returned to the Lord, according to that of the apostle, Col. iii. 16.

But as to their artificial musick, either by organs, or other instruments, or voice, we have neither example nor precept for it in the New Testament.

Baptism

As there is one Lord, and one faith, so there is one baptism; which is not the putting away the filth of the flesh, but the answer of a good conscience before God, by the resurrection of Jesus Christ. And this baptism is a pure and spiritual thing, to wit, the baptism of the Spirit and Fire, by which we are buried with him, that being washed and purged from our sins, we may walk in newness of life: of which the baptism of John was a figure, which was commanded for a time, and not to continue for ever. As to the baptism of infants, it is a mere human tradition, for which neither precept nor practice is to be found in all the scripture.

That the one baptism of Christ is not a washing with water, appears from I Pet. iii. 21. *The like figure whereunto even baptism doth also now save us (not the putting away of the filth of the flesh, but the answer of a good conscience towards God) by the resurrection of Jesus Christ.* So plain a definition of baptism is not in all the bible; and therefore, seeing it so plain, it may well be preferred to all the coined definitions of the schoolmen. He saith not that it is the water, or the putting away of the filth of the flesh, as accompanied with the answer of a good conscience, whereof the one, viz., water, is the sacramental element, administered by the minister; and the other, the grace or thing signified, conferred by Christ; but plainly, That it is not the putting away, &c. than which there can be nothing more manifest to men unprejudicate and judicious. For seeing we are saved by this baptism, as all those that were in the ark were saved by water, it would then follow, that all those that have this baptism are saved by it. Now this consequence would be false, if it were understood of water-baptism; because many, by the confession of all, are baptized with water that are not saved; but this consequence holds most true, if it be understood as we do, of the baptism of the Spirit; since none can have this answer of a good conscience, and, abiding in it, not be saved by it.

For it is not outward washing with water that maketh the heart clean, by which men are fitted for heaven: and as that which goeth into the mouth doth not defile a man, because it is put forth again, and so goeth to the dunghill; neither doth any thing which man eateth purify him, or fit him for heaven.

Communion

The communion of the body and blood of Christ is in-

83

ward and spiritual, which is the participation of his flesh and blood, by which the inward man is daily nourished in the hearts of those in whom Christ dwells. Of which things the breaking of bread by Christ with his disciples was a figure, which even they who had received the substance used in the church for a time, for the sake of the weak; even as abstaining from things strangled, and from blood, the washing of one another's feet, and the anointing of the sick with oil: all which are commanded with no less authority and solemnity than the former; yet seeing they are but shadows of better things, they cease in such as have obtained the substance.

Lastly, If any now at this day, from a true tenderness of spirit, and with real conscience towards God, did practise this ceremony in the same way, method, and manner as did the primitive Christians recorded in scripture, I should not doubt to affirm but they might be indulged in it, and the Lord might regard them, and for a season appear to them in the use of these things, as many of us have known him to do to us in the time of our ignorance; providing always they did not seek to obtrude them upon others, nor judge such as found themselves delivered from them, or that they do not pertinaciously adhere to them. For we certainly know that the day is dawned, in which God hath arisen, and hath dismissed all those ceremonies and rites, and is only to be worshipped in Spirit, and that he appears to them who wait upon him; and that to seek God in these things is, with Mary at the sepulchre, to seek the living among the dead: for we know that he is risen, and revealed in Spirit, leading his children out of these rudiments, that they may walk with him in his light; to whom be glory for ever. Amen.

III. TESTIMONIES

HAVING hitherto treated of the principles of religion, both relating to doctrine and worship, I am now to speak of some practices which have been the product of this principle, in those witnesses whom God hath raised up in this day to testify for his truth. It will not a little commend them, I suppose, in the judgment of sober and judicious men, that taking them generally, even by the confession of their adversaries, they are found to be free of those abominations which abound among other professors, such as are swearing, drunkenness, whoredom, riotousness, &c, and that generally the very coming among those people doth naturally work such a change, so that many vicious and profane persons have been known, by coming to this truth, to become sober and virtuous.

But there are some singular things, which most of all our adversaries plead for the lawfulness of, and allow themselves in, as no ways inconsistent with the Christian religion, which we have found to be no ways lawful unto us, and have been commanded of the Lord to lay them aside; tho' the doing thereof hath occasioned no small sufferings and buffetings, and hath procured us much hatred and malice from the world. And because the nature of these things is such, that they do upon the very sight distinguish us, and make us known, so that we cannot hide ourselves from any, without proving unfaithful to our testimony; our trials and exercises have herethrough proved the more numerous and difficult, as will after appear.

I would not have any judge, that hereby we intend to destroy the mutual relation that either is betwixt prince and people, master and servants, parents and children; nay, not at all: we shall evidence, that our principle in these things hath no such tendency, and that these natural relations are rather better established, than any ways hurt by it. Next, Let not any judge, that from our opinion in these things, any necessity of levelling will follow, or that all men must have things in common. Our principle leaves every man to enjoy that peaceably, which either his own industry, or his parents, have purchased to him; only he is thereby instructed to use it aright, both for his own good, and that of his brethren; and all to the Glory of God: in which also his acts are to be voluntary, and no ways constrained.

These things premised, I would seriously propose unto all such, as choose to be Christians indeed, and that in nature, and not in name only whether it were not desirable, and would not greatly contribute to the commendation of Christianity, and to the increase of the life and virtue of Christ, if all superfluous titles of honour, profuseness and prodigality in meat and apparel, gaming, sporting and playing, were laid aside and forborne? And whether such as lay them aside, in so doing, walk not more like the disciples of Christ and his apostles, and are therein nearer their example, than such as use them? Certainly the sober and serious among all sorts will say, Yea. And God hath made it manifest in this age, that by discovering the evil of such things, and leading his witnesses out of them, and to testify against them, he hath produced effectually in many that mortification and abstraction from the love and cares of this world, who daily are conversing in the world (but inwardly redeemed out of it) both in wedlock, and in their lawful employments, which was judged could only be obtained by such as were shut up in cloisters and monasteries. Thus much in general.

Titles

We affirm positively, That it is not lawful for Christians either to give or receive titles of honour, as, Your Holiness, Your Majesty, Your Excellency, Your Eminency, &c.

First, Because these titles are no part of that obedience which is due to magistrates or superiors; neither doth the giving them add to or diminish from that subjection we owe to them, which consists in obeying their just and lawful commands, not in titles and designations.

For if these titles arise either from the office or worth of the persons, it will not be denied, but the apostles deserved them better than any now that call for them. But the case is plain, the apostles had the holiness, the excellency, the grace; and because they were holy, excellent, and gracious, they neither used, nor admitted of such titles.

Lastly, All these titles and stiles of honour are to be rejected by Christians, because they are to seek the honour that comes from above, and not the honour that is from below: but these honours are not that honour that comes from above, but are from below.

It will not be unfit in this place to say something concerning the using of the singular number to one person; of this there is no controversy in the Latin. For when we speak to one, we always use the pronoun TU and he that would do otherwise would break the rules of grammar, concerning which likewise James Howel, in his epistle to the nobility of England, before the French and English Dictionary, takes notice, that both in France, and in other nations, the word THOU was used in speaking to one; but by succession of time, when the Roman commonwealth grew into an empire, the courtiers began to magnify the emperor, (as being furnished with power to confer dignities and offices) using the word YOU, yea, and deifying him with more remarkable titles. So that the word YOU in the plural number, together with the other titles and compellations of honour, seem to have taken their rise from monarchial government; which afterwards, by degrees, came to be derived to private persons.

Moreover that this way of speaking proceeds from an high and proud mind, hence appears; because that men commonly use the singular number to beggars, and to their servants; yea and in their prayers to God. Thus the superior will speak to his inferior, who yet will not bear that the inferior so speak to him, as judging it a kind of reproach unto him. So hath the pride of men placed God and the beggar in the same category. Seeing therefore it is manifest to us, that this form of speaking to men in the plural number doth proceed from pride, as well as that it is in itself a lie, we found the necessity upon us to testify against this corruption, by using the singular equally unto all.

Hat and Knee

Secondly, Next unto this of titles, the other part of honour used among Christians in the kneeling, bowing, and uncovering of the head to one another.

First, We say, That God, who is the Creator of man, and he to whom he oweth the dedication both of soul and body, is over all to be worshipped and adored, and that not only by the spirit, but also with the prostration of body. Now kneeling, bowing, and uncovering of the head, is the alone outward signification of our adoration towards God, and therefore it is not lawful to give it unto man. He that kneeleth, or prostrates himself to man, what doth he more to God? He that boweth, and uncovereth his head to the creature, what hath he reserved to the Creator?

Secondly, Men being alike by creation (though their being stated under their several relations requires from them mutual services according to those respective relations) owe not worship one to another, but all equally are to return it to God. All men, by an inward instinct, in all nations have been led to prostrate and bow themselves to God. And it is plain that this bowing to men took place from a slavish fear possessing some, which led them to set up others as gods; when also an ambitious proud spirit got up in those others, to usurp the place of God over their brethren.

And forasmuch as they accuse us herein of rudeness and pride, though the testimony of our consciences in the sight of God be a sufficient guard against such calumnies, yet there are of us known to be men of such education, as forbear not these things for want of that they call good breeding; and we should be very void of reason, to purchase that pride at so dear a rate, as many have done the exercise of their conscience in this matter; many of us having been sorely beaten and buffeted, yea, and several months imprisoned, for no other reason but because we could not so satisfy the proud unreasonable humours of proud men, as to uncover our heads, and bow our bodies. Nor doth our innocent practice, in standing still, though upright, not putting off our hats, any more than our shoes, the one being the covering of our heads, as well as the other of our feet, shew so much rudeness, as their beating and knocking us, &c. because we cannot bow to them, contrary to our consciences: which certainly shews less meekness and humility upon their part, than it doth of rudeness or pride upon ours. And this I can say boldly, in the sight of God, from my own experience, and that of many thousands more, that however small or foolish this may seem, yet we behoved to choose death rather than do it, and that for conscience sake: and that in its being so contrary to our natural spirits, there are many of us, to whom the forsaking of these bowings and ceremonies was as death itself; which we could never have left, if we could have enjoyed our peace with God in the use of them.

Apparel

The third thing to be treated of, is the vanity and superfluity of apparel. In which, first, two things are to be considered, the condition of the person, and country he lives in. We shall not say that all persons are to be clothed alike, because it will perhaps neither suit their bodies nor their estates. And if a man be clothed soberly, and without superfluity, tho' they may be finer than that which his servant is clothed with, we shall not blame him for it: the abstaining from superfluities, which his condition and education have accustomed him to, may be in him a greater act of mortification than the abstaining from finer clothes in the servant, who never was accustomed to them. As to the country, what it naturally produces may be no vanity to the inhabitants to use, or what is commonly imparted to them by way of exchange, seeing it is without doubt that the creation is for the use of man. So where silk abounds, it may be worn as well as wool; and were we in those countries, or near unto them, where gold or silver were as common as iron or brass, the one might be used as well as the other. The iniquity lies then here, First, When from a lust of vanity, and a desire to adorn themselves, men and women, not content with what their condition can bear, or their country easily affords, do stretch to have things, that from their rarity, and the price that is put upon them, seem to be precious, and so feed their lust the more; and this all sober men of all sorts will readily grant to be evil.

Gaming

Fourthly, Let us consider the use of games, sports, comedies, and other such things, commonly and indifferently used by all the several sorts of Christians, under the notion of divertisement and recreation, and see whether these things can consist with the seriousness, gravity, and Godly fear, which the gospel calls for.

There is no duty more frequently commanded, nor more incumbent upon Christians, than the fear of the Lord, to stand in awe before him, to walk as in his presence; but if such as use these games and sports will speak from their consciences, they can, I doubt not, experimentally declare, that this fear is forgotten in their gaming: and if God by this light secretly touch them, or mind them of the vanity of their way, they strive to shut it out, and use their gaming as an engine to put away from them that troublesome guest.

But they object, That men's spirits could not subsist, if they were always intent upon serious and spiritual matters, and that therefore there is need of some divertisement to recreate the mind a little, whereby it being refreshed, is able with great vigour to apply itself to these things.

I answer; Though all this were granted, it would no ways militate against us, neither plead the use of these things, which we would have wholly laid aside. For that men should be always in the same intentiveness of mind, we do not plead, knowing how impossible it is, so long as we are clothed with this tabernacle of clay. But this will not allow us at any time to recede from the remembrance of God, and of our souls' chief concern, as not still to retain a certain sense of his fear; which cannot be so much as rationally supposed to be in the use of these things which we condemn. Now the necessary occasions in which all are involved, in order to the care and sustentation of the outward man, are a relaxation of the mind from the more serious duties; and those are performed in the blessing, as the mind is so leavened with the love of God, and the sense of his presence, that even in doing these things the soul carrieth with it that divine influence and spiritual habit, whereby though these acts, as of eating, drinking, sleeping, working, be upon the matter one with what the wicked do, yet they are done in another Spirit; and in doing of them we please the Lord, serve him, and answer our end in the creation, and so feel and are sensible of his blessing. There are innocent divertisements which may sufficiently serve for relaxation of the mind, such as for friends to visit one another; to hear or read history; to speak soberly of the present or past transactions; to follow after gardening; to use geometrical and mathematical experiments, and such other things of this nature. In all which things we are not to forget God, in whom we both live, and are moved, Acts xvii. 28. as not to have always some secret reserve to him, and sense of his fear and presence; which also frequently exerts itself in the midst of these things by some short aspiration and breathings.

Swearing

Fifthly, The use of swearing is to be considered, which is so frequently practised almost among all Christians; not only profane oaths among the profane, in their common discourses, whereby the Most HOLY NAME of GOD is in a horrible manner daily blasphemed; but also solemn oaths with those that have some shew of piety, whereof the most part do defend swearing before the magistrate with so great zeal, that not only they are ready themselves to do it upon every occasion, but also have stirred up the magistrates to persecute those, who, out of obedience to Christ, their Lord and master, judge it unlawful to swear; upon which account not a few have suffered imprisonment, and the spoiling of their goods.

But considering these clear words of our Saviour, Mat. v. 33, 34. *Again, ye have heard that it hath been said by them of old time, Thou shalt not forswear thyself, but shall perform unto the Lord thine oaths. But I say unto you, SWEAR NOT AT ALL, neither by heaven, &c. But let your communication be yea, yea; nay, nay; for whatsoever is more than these cometh of evil.* As also the words of the apostle James, v. 12. *But above all things, my brethren, swear not, neither by heaven, neither by the earth, neither by any other oath; but let your yea be yea, and your nay, nay lest ye fall into condemnation.*

It is no ways lawful for a Christian to swear, whom Christ has called to his essential truth, which was before all oaths, forbidding him to swear; and on the contrary, commanding him to speak the truth in all things; to the honour of Christ who called him; that it may appear that the words of his disciples may be as truly believed as the oaths of all the worldy men. Neither is it lawful for them to be unfaithful in this, that they may please others, or that they may avoid their hurt: for thus the primitive Christians for some ages remained faithful, who being required to swear, did unanimously answer, I am a Christian, I do not swear.

Who then needs further to doubt, but that since Christ would have his disciples attain the highest pitch of perfection, he abrogated oaths, as a rudiment of infirmity, and in place thereof established the use of truth?

Fighting

Sixthly, The last thing to be considered, is revenge and war, an evil as opposite and contrary to the Spirit and doctrine of Christ as light to darkness. For through contempt of Christ's law the whole world is filled with violence, oppression, murders, ravishing of women and virgins, spoilings, depredations, and all manner of lasciviousness and cruelty: so that it is strange that men, made after the image of God, should have so much degenerated, that they rather bear the image and nature of roaring lions, tearing tigers, devouring wolves, and raging boars, than of rational creatures endued with reason. And is it not yet much more admirable,* that this horrid monster should find place, and be fomented, among those men that profess themselves disciples of our peaceable Lord and master Jesus Christ, who by excellency is called the Prince of Peace, and hath expressly prohibited his children all violence; and on the contrary, commanded them, that, according to his example, they should follow patience, charity, forbearance, and other virtues worthy of a Christian?

Hear then what this great prophet saith, whom every soul is commanded to hear, under the pain of being cut off, Mat. v. from verse 38 to the end of the chapter. For thus he saith: *Ye have heard that it hath been said, An eye for an eye, and a tooth for a tooth: But I say unto you, That ye resist not evil; but whosoever shall smite thee on thy right check, turn to him the other also. And if any man will sue thee at the law, and take away thy coat, let him have thy cloak also. And whosoever shall compel thee to go a mile, go with him twain. Give to him that asketh thee; and from him that would borrow of thee, turn not thou away. Ye have heard that it has been said, Thou shalt love thy neighbor, and hate thine enemy: but I say unto you, Love your enemies, bless them that curse you, do good to them that hate you, and pray for them which despitefully use you, and persecute*

---

* To be wondered at.

you, that ye may be the children of your Father which is in heaven. For he maketh his sun to rise on the evil and on the good, and sendeth rain on the just and on the unjust For if ye love them which love you, what reward have ye? Do not even the Publicans the same? And if ye salute your brethren only, what do you more than others? Do not even the Publicans so? Be ye therefore perfect, even as your Father which is in heaven is perfect.

And truly the words are so clear in themselves, that, in my judgment, they need no illustration to explain their sense: for it is as easy to reconcile the greatest contradictions, as these laws of our Lord Jesus Christ with the wicked practices of wars; for they are plainly inconsistent. Whoever can reconcile this, Resist not evil, with resist violence by force: again, Give also thy other cheek, with strike again; also Love thine enemies, with spoil them, make a prey of them, pursue them with fire and sword; or Pray for those that persecute you, and those that calumniate you, with persecute them by fines, imprisonments, and death itself; and not only such as do not persecute you, but who heartily seek and desire your eternal and temporal welfare: whoever, I say, can find a means to reconcile these things, may be supposed also to have found a way to reconcile God with the devil, Christ with Antichrist, light with darkness, and good with evil.

These words, with respect to revenge, as the former in the case of swearing, do forbid some things, which in time past were lawful to the Jews, considering their condition and dispensation; and command unto such as will be the disciples of Christ, a more perfect, eminent, and full signification of charity, as also patience and suffering, than was required of them in that time, state, and dispensation by the law of Moses. This is not only the judgment of most, if not all, the ancient fathers, so called, of the first three hundred years after Christ, but also of many others.

Two or three ages afterwards Christians altogether rejected war if the emperor Marc. Aurel. Anton. be to be credited, who writes thus:—*I prayed to my country gods; but when I was neglected by them, and observed myself pressed by the enemy, considering the fewness of my forces, I called to one, and intreated those who with us are called Christians, and I found a great number of them; and I forced them with threats, which ought not to have been, because afterwards I knew their strength and force: therefore they betook themselves neither to the use of darts nor trumpets, for they use not so to do, for the cause and name of their God, which they bear in their consciences:* and this was done about an hundred and sixty years after Christ. To this add those words, which in Justin Martyr the Christians answer, *We fight not with our enemies.* And moreover the answer of Martin to Julian the apostate, related by Sulpitius Severus, *I am a soldier of Christ, therefore I cannot fight:* which was three hundred years after Christ.

And James tells us, that fighting proceeds from the lusts. So that it were fitter for Christians, by the sword of God's Spirit, to fight against their lusts, than by the prevalency of their lusts to destroy one another. Whatever honour any might have attained of old under the Law this way, we find under the Gospel Christians commended for suffering, not for fighting; neither did any of Christ's disciples, save one, offer outward violence by the sword, in cutting off Malchus's ear; for which he received no title of honour, but a just reproof.

And although this thing be so much known, yet it is as well known that almost all the modern sects live in the neglect and contempt of this law of Christ, and likewise

oppress others, who in this agree not with them for conscience sake towards God: even as we have suffered much in
our country, because we neither could ourselves bear arms;
nor send others in our place, nor give our money for the
buying of drums, standards, and other military attire. And
lastly, Because we could not hold our doors, windows, and
shops close, for conscience sake, upon such days as fasts and
prayers were appointed, to desire a blessing upon, and success for, the arms of the kingdom or commonwealth under
which we live; neither give thanks for the victories acquired
by the effusion of much blood. By which forcing of the conscience, they would have constrained our brethren, living in
divers kingdoms at war together, to have implored our God
for contrary and contradictory things, and consequentially
impossible; for it is impossible that two parties fighting
together, should both obtain the victory.

They object, That Christ, Luke xxii. 36. speaking to his
disciples, commands them, That he that then had not a
sword, should sell his coat, and buy a sword; therefore, say
they, arms are lawful.

I answer, Some indeed understand this of the outward
sword, nevertheless regarding only that occasion; otherwise
judging, that Christians are prohibited wars under the
gospel. Among which is Ambrose, who upon this place
speaks thus: *O Lord; why commandest thou me to buy a
sword, who forbiddest me to smite with it? Why commandest thou me to have it, whom thou prohibitest to draw it?
Unless perhaps a defence be prepared, not a necessary revenge; and that I may seem to have been able to revenge,
but that I would not.* Others judge Christ to have spoken
here mystically, and not according to the letter. And truly
when we consider the answer of the disciples, Master, behold here are two swords; understanding it of outward

swords; and again Christ's answer, It is enough; it seems that Christ would not that the rest, who had not swords (for they had only two swords) should sell their coats, and buy an outward sword. Who can think that, matters standing thus, he should have said, Two was enough?

They object, That the scriptures and old fathers, so called, did only prohibit private revenge, not the use of arms for the defence of our country, body, wives, children, and goods, when the magistrate commands it, seeing the magistrate ought to be obeyed; therefore although it be not lawful for private men to do it of themselves, nevertheless they are bound to do it by the command of the magistrate.

I answer, If the magistrate be truly a Christian, or desire to be so, he ought himself, in the first place, to obey the command of his master, saying, Love your enemies, &c. and then he could not command us to kill them; but if he be not a true Christian, then ought we to obey our Lord and King, Jesus Christ, whom he ought also to obey: for in the kingdom of Christ all ought to submit to his laws, from the highest to the lowest, that is, from the king to the beggar, and from Caesar to the clown.

They object, That defence is of natural right, and that religion destroys not nature.

I answer, Be it so; but to obey God, and commend ourselves to him in faith and patience, is not to destroy nature, but to exalt and perfect it; to wit, to elevate it from the natural to the supernatural life, by Christ living therein, and comforting it, that it may do all things, and be rendered more than conqueror.

But lastly, as to what relates to this thing, since nothing seems more contrary to man's nature, and seeing of all things the defence of one's self seems most tolerable, as it is most hard to men, so it is the most perfect part of the Christian religion, as that wherein the denial of self and entire confidence in God doth most appear; and therefore Christ and his apostles left us hereof a most perfect example. As to what relates to the present magistrates of the Christian world, albeit we deny them not altogether the name of Christians, because of the publick profession they make of Christ's name, yet we may boldly affirm, that they are far from the perfection of the Christian religion; because in the state in which they are (as in many places before I have largely observed) they have not come to the pure dispensation of the gospel. And therefore, while they are in that condition, we shall not say, That war, undertaken upon a just occasion, is altogether unlawful to them. For even as circumcision and the other ceremonies were for a season permitted to the Jews, not because they were either necessary of themselves, or lawful at that time, after the resurrection of Christ, but because that Spirit was not yet raised up in them, whereby they could be delivered from such rudiments; so the present confessors of the Christian name, who are yet in the mixture, and not in the patient suffering spirit, are not yet fitted for this form of Christianity, and therefore cannot be undefending themselves until they attain that perfection. But for such whom Christ has brought hither, it is not lawful to defend themselves by arms, but they ought over all to trust to the Lord.

Liberty of Conscience

Liberty of conscience from the power of the civil magistrate hath been of late years so largely and learnedly handled, that I shall need to be but brief in it; yet it is to be lamented that few have walked answerably to this principle, each pleading it for themselves, but scarce allowing it to others.

That no man, by virtue of any power or principality he hath in the government of this world, hath power over the consciences of men, is apparent, because the conscience of man is the seat and throne of God in him, of which God is the alone proper and infallible judge, who by his power and Spirit can alone rectify the mistakes of conscience, and therefore hath reserved to himself the power of punishing the errors thereof as he seeth meet.

We understand by matters of conscience such as immediately relate betwixt God and man, or men and men, that are under the same persuasion, as to meet together and worship God in that way which they judge is most acceptable unto him, and not to encroach upon, or seek to force their neighbours, otherwise than by reason, or such other means as Christ and his apostles used, viz. Preaching and instructing such as will hear and receive it; but not at all for men, under the notion of conscience, to do any thing contrary to the moral and perpetual statutes generally acknowledged by all Christians; in which case the magistrate may very lawfully use his authority; as on those, who, under a pretence of conscience, make it a principle to kill and destroy all the wicked, *id est,* all that differ from them that they, to wit, the saints, may rule. But the liberty we lay claim to is such as the primitive church justly sought under the heathen emperors, to wit, for men of sobriety, honesty, and a peaceable conversation, to enjoy the liberty and exercise of their conscience towards God and among themselves, and to admit among them such as by their persuasion and influence come to be convinced of the same truth with them, without being therefore molested by the civil magistrate. Though we would not have men hurt in their temporals, nor robbed of their privileges as men and members of the commonwealth, because of their inward persuasion; yet we are far from judging that in the church of God there should not be censures exercised against such as fall into error, as well as such as commit open evils; and therefore we believe it may be very lawful for a Christian church, if she find any of her members fall into any error, after due admonitions and instructions according to gospel order, if she find them pertinacious, to cut them off from her fellowship by the sword of the Spirit, and deprive them of those privileges which they had as fellow-members; but not to cut them off from the world by the temporal sword, or rob them of their common privileges as men, seeing they enjoy not these as Christians, or under such a fellowship, but as men, and members of the creation. Hence Chrysostom saith well, (de Anath.) *We must condemn and reprove the evil doctrines that proceed from Hereticks; but spare the men, and pray for their salvation.*

And it is observable, that notwithstanding many other superstitions crept into the church very early, yet this of persecution was so inconsistent with the nature of the gospel, and liberty of conscience, as we have asserted it, such an innate and natural part of the Christian religion, that almost all the Christian writers, for the first three hundred years, earnestly contended for it, condemning the contrary opinion.

Now the ground of persecution is an unwillingness to suffer; for no man, that will persecute another for his conscience, would suffer for his own, if he could avoid it, seeing his principle obliges him, if he had power, by force to establish that which he judges is the truth, and so to force others to it. Therefore I judge it meet, for the information of the nations, briefly to add something in this place concerning the nature of true Christian sufferings, whereunto a very faithful testimony hath been borne by God's witnesses.

101

Of this excellent patience and sufferings, the witnesses of God, in scorn called Quakers, have given a manifest proof: for so soon as God revealed his truth among them, without regard to any opposition whatsoever, or what they might meet with, they went up and down, as they were moved of the Lord, preaching and propagating the truth in market-places, highways, streets, and publick temples, though daily beaten, whipped, bruised, haled, and imprisoned therefore. And when there was any where a church or assembly gathered, they taught them to keep their meetings openly, and not to shut the door, nor do it by stealth, that all might know it, and those who would might enter. And hereby all just occasion of fear of plotting against the government was fully removed, so this their courage and faithfulness in not giving over their meeting together (but more especially the presence and glory of God manifested in the meeting being terrible to the consciences of the persecutors) did so weary out the malice of their adversaries, that oftentimes they were forced to leave their work undone. For when they came to break up a meeting, they were obliged to take every individual out by force, they not being free to give up their liberty by dissolving at their command: and when they were haled out, unless they were kept forth by violence, they presently returned peaceably to their place. Yea, when sometimes the magistrates have pulled down their meeting houses, they have met the next day openly upon the rubbish, and so by innocency kept their possession and ground, being properly their own, and their right to meet and worship God being not forfeited to any.

The true, faithful and Christian suffering is for men to profess what they are persuaded is right, and so practise and perform their worship towards God, as being their true right so to do; and neither to do more in that, because of outward encouragement from men; nor any whit less, because of the fear of their laws and acts against it. Thus for a Christian man to vindicate his just liberty with so much boldness, and yet innocency, will in due time, though through blood, purchase peace, as this age hath in some measure experienced, and many are witnesses of it; which yet shall be more apparent to the world, as truth takes place on earth. But they greatly sin against this excellent rule, that in time of persecution do not profess their own way so much as they would if it were otherwise; and yet, when they can get the magistrate upon their side, not only stretch their own liberty to the utmost, but seek to establish the same by denying it to others.

Now against our unparalleled yet innocent and Christian cause our malicious enemies have nothing to say, but that if we had power, we would do likewise. This is a piece of mere unreasonable malice, and a privilege they take to judge of things to come, which they have not by immediate revelation; and surely it is the greatest height of harsh judgment to say men would do contrary to their professed principle if they could, who have from their practice hitherto given no ground for it, and wherein they only judge others by themselves: such conjectures cannot militate against us, so long as we are innocent. And if ever we prove guilty of persecution, by forcing other men by corporal punishment to our way, then let us be judged the greatest of hypocrites, and let not any spare to persecute us. Amen, saith my soul.

THE CONCLUSION

IF IN God's fear, candid reader, thou appliest thyself to consider this system of religion here delivered, with its consistency and harmony, as well in itself as with the scriptures of truth, I doubt not but thou wilt say with me and many more, that this is the spiritual day of Christ's appearance, wherein he is again revealing the ancient paths of truth and righteousness. For which end he hath called us to be a first fruits of those that serve him, and worship him no more in the oldness of the letter, but in the newness of the Spirit. And though we be few in number, in respect of others, and weak as to outward strength, which we also altogether reject, and foolish if compared with the wise ones of this world; yet as God hath prospered us, notwithstanding much opposition, so will he yet do, that neither the art, wisdom, nor violence of men or devils shall be able to quench that little spark that hath appeared; but it shall grow to the consuming of whatsoever shall stand up to oppose it! yea, he that hath arisen in a small remnant shall arise and go on by the same arm of power in his spiritual manifestation, until he hath conquered all his enemies, until all the kingdoms of the earth become the kingdom of Christ Jesus.

DISCUSSION QUESTIONS FOR *BARCLAY IN BRIEF**

BELIEF

Immediate Revelation
1. What, to Barclay, is the distinction between natural and spiritual, and the characteristics of each?
2. Barclay says spiritual knowledge is certain and evident: in what sense? How do you contrast with scientific knowledge?
3. How would Barclay answer a skeptic who denied such spiritual knowledge? What would *you* say?

The Scriptures
1. How would Barclay test the authenticity of inspiration, distinguishing it from insane or "demonic" impulses?
2. What would Barclay say to the argument that inspiration needs to be tested by an objective standard like the Scriptures?
3. How does Barclay himself use Scriptural authority? How do *you* think we should use it?

The Condition of Man in the Fall
1. Why does Barclay reject the concept of "original sin"?
2. How would you compare Barclay's description of sinfulness with modern conceptions of man's alienation?
3. How deep does he think man's sinfulness goes? What would *you* say?

Universal and Saving Light
1. A bishop once said: "There are only two Christians in Detroit, and they are both Jews." How does this compare with Barclay's statement of the universality of Christ? Who today would qualify as Christians in this larger sense?
2. What place, if any, does Barclay find for the life and work of the historical Jesus?
3. How does Barclay deal with the problem of freedom of the will?

Reason, Conscience
1. What for Barclay is the place of reason? What do *you* think?
2. How would Barclay answer those who say all morality is culture-conditioned and relative?

Justification, Perfection
1. The doctrine of justification by faith is supposed to avoid moralism—good works as qualification for God's grace. How well does Barclay avoid such moralism?
2. How would Barclay meet Niebuhr's argument that all men have an irreducible core of self-centeredness? How far can men be liberated from sinfulness?

---

*Prepared by Carol R. Murphy

Nature of the Church
What is the basis of true church membership, according to Barclay?

Worship, Ministry
1. Calvin said that man's mind is an idol-making factory. To what extent would Barclay agree that much of what we call religion is really sin?
2. Why do you think many Meetings no longer seem to produce the profound spiritual experiences Barclay describes?
3. What would Barclay say to a modern pastor who argues that his is a full-time job requiring a knowledge of pastoral counseling, religious education, problems of urban environments, etc.? To what extent, if any, do Barclay's views need adaptation to the complexities of modern life?
4. What, to Barclay, is the relation between inward prayer and outward expression? How would he judge spiritual exercises or yogas?

The Sacraments: Baptism and Communion
Granted that the reality lies in the Spirit behind the forms, to what extent can the Spirit be real *to us* without outward expression? How have such outward expressions helped or hindered your own spiritual exercises?

TESTIMONIES

Titles and Honors
1. To what extent might disregard of signs of social status be more revolutionary in result than Barclay allows for?
2. How may one prevent such disregard from becoming sheer bad manners?

Gaming, Swearing
1. What would Barclay think of today's TV programming? What kinds of recreation today would meet his approval?
2. What for Barclay is the true guarantee of truthfulness? What would Barclay say about loyalty oaths?

Fighting
How would Barclay deal with non-pacifist "realists" like Niebuhr who feel that not perfection, but the lesser evil, is our only choice?

Liberty of Conscience
What are the bounds Barclay sets on liberty to live by one's conscience? How would he deal with radicals of right or left who do not recognize freedom for others to differ? What would be *your* solution?

106

THE INWARD JOURNEY OF
ISAAC PENINGTON

AN ABBREVIATION OF PENINGTON'S WORKS

BY

ROBERT J. LEACH

PENDLE HILL PAMPHLET 29

He that readeth these things, let him not strive to comprehend them; but be content with what he feeleth thereof suitable to his own present estate, and as the life grows in him, and he in the life . . . the words . . . will of themselves open to him.

ISAAC PENINGTON

INTRODUCTION

THE spiritual writings of Isaac Penington (1617-1679) evoke a real response in our present troubled world. Their advice concerning the slow growth of inward comprehension speaks to our condition. Penington's many short pamphlets upon religious subjects were collected and published after the death of their author, in a folio volume entitled:

> The Works of the Long-Mournful and Sorely-Distressed Isaac Penington, whom the Lord in his Tender Mercy, at length Visited and Relieved by the Ministry of that Despised People, called Quakers; and in the Springings of that Light, Life and Holy Power in him, which they had Truly and Faithfully Testified of, and Directed his mind to, were these things Written, and are now Published as a thankful Testimony of the goodness of the Lord unto him, and for the Benefit of others.

This first edition, of 1681, has been several times republished and a number of books of selections have been edited. These are now out of print. For this reason the crystal-clear purity of Isaac Penington's heavenly cadences is scarcely available to any but scholars.

The *Inward Journey of Isaac Penington* is an abbreviation of the 1,400 pages of the second London edition of 1761. The extracted portions have been joined to form a sequence. The deepest questions are asked and answered: What of thee? Art thou in thine own soul's true rest? What is the seed, or portion of God in every heart? What of free will, justification, perfection, and more especially, love, joy, and peace? The lyric beauty of Penington's free verse carries the reader along to the subject of public worship, in which Christ himself speaks.

Half of Isaac Penington's twenty-two Quaker years were spent in prison—"in outward bonds for Christ's sake." At first hand he knew of the blessed community, of the persecuting spirit, and of men's dependence upon war and violence. After dealing with Quaker testimonies, the *Inward Journey* recapitulates the steps by which all may find the living virtue which Isaac Penington had himself discovered and which brought him the sense of salvation.

A few additional facts concerning Penington's life should be noted. Born in 1617, son of Alderman Isaac Penington, a distinguished Puritan who was at one time Lord Mayor of London, he received an excellent education which was reflected in his able use of the English tongue. A fashionable fling in London society eventuated in his marriage to Lady Mary Springett whose daughter by a prior marriage was later to become the wife of William Penn. In 1658 the Peningtons, who had long been religious seekers, fully associated themselves with the then new Society of Friends. Rejecting their worldly advantages, they became consistent and fervent members of the new spiritual movement. As public Friends and ministers of God's holy word, Isaac Penington and his wife travelled in the company of James Naylor, George Keith, William Penn, George Fox, and Robert Barclay. In the *Inward Journey* we participate in this flood-tide of Christian experience. We become "tinctured" by the authenticity of the witness that is here recorded. We should be, in a measure, revitalized by means of Isaac Penington's heavenly words.

1

THE SPRING OF LIFE

I WAS acquainted with a spring of life from my childhood, which enlightened me in my tender years and pointed my heart towards the Lord, begetting true sense in me, and faith, and hope, and love, and humility, and meekness, . . . so that indeed I was a wonder to some that knew me, because of the savor and life of religion which dwelt in my heart and appeared in my conversation.

But I never durst trust the spring of my life, . . . but, in reading the Scriptures, gathered what knowledge I could therefrom, and set this over the spring and springings of life in me, and indeed judged that I ought so to do.

Indeed, I did not look to have been so broken, shattered, and distressed as I afterwards was, and could by no means understand the meaning thereof, . . . not having the sense of any guilt upon me. Divers came to see me, some to enquire into, and consider of, my condition; others to bewail it and (if possible) administer some relief, help, and comfort to me; and divers were the judgments they had concerning me. Some would say it was deep melancholy; others would narrowly search and enquire how, and in what manner, . . . I had walked; and were jealous that I had sinned against the Lord and provoked him some way or other, and that some iniquity lay as a load upon me; but, after thorough converse with me, they would still express that they were of another mind and that the hand of the Lord was in it, . . . and it would end in good to my soul.

When I was broken and dashed to pieces in my religion, I was in a congregational way; but soon after parted with them, yet in great love, relating to them how the hand of the Lord was upon me, and how I was smitten in the inward part of my religion, and could not now hold up an outward form of that which I inwardly wanted, having lost my God, my Christ, my faith, my knowledge, my life, my all. And so we parted very lovingly, I wishing them well, even the presence of that God whom I wanted; promising to return to them again, if ever I met with that which my soul wanted, and had clearness in the Lord so to do.

In this great trouble and grief, . . . and in mourning over and grappling with secret corruptions and temptations, I spent many years. and fell into great weakness of body; and often casting myself upon my bed, did wring my hands and weep bitterly, begging earnestly of the Lord, daily, that I might be pitied by him, and helped against my enemies, and be made conformable to the image of his Son, by his own renewing power. And indeed at last (when my nature was almost spent, and the pit of despair was even closing its mouth upon me) mercy sprang, and deliverance came, and the Lord my God owned me, and sealed his love unto me, and light sprang within me, which made not only the Scriptures. but the very outward creatures glorious in my eye, so that everything was sweet and pleasant and lightsome round about me. But I soon felt that this estate was too high and glorious for me, and I was not able to abide in it, it so overcame my natural spirits; wherefore, blessing the name of the Lord for his great goodness to me, I prayed unto him to take that from me which I was not able to bear, and to give me such a proportion of his light and presence as was suitable to my present state, and might fit me for his service. Whereupon this was presently removed from me, yet a savor remained with me, wherein I had sweetness, and comfort, and refreshment for a long season.

"Well then, how came this about?" will some say.

Why thus. The Lord opened my spirit, the Lord gave me the certain and sensible feeling of the pure seed, which had been with me from the beginning; the Lord caused his holy power to fall upon me, and gave me such an inward demonstration and feeling of the seed of life, that I cried out in my spirit, *This is he, this is he; there is not another, there never was another. He was always near me, though I knew him not. . . . Oh! that I might now be joined to him, and he alone might live in me.* And so in the willingness which God had wrought in me. . . I gave up to be instructed, exercised, and led by him, in the waiting for and feeling of his holy seed, that all might be wrought out of me which could not live with the seed . . . . And so I have gone through a sore travail and fight of afflictions and temptations of many kinds, wherein the Lord hath been merciful to me in helping me and preserving the spark of life in me, in the midst of many things which had befallen me, whose nature tended to quench and extinguish it.

Now thus having met with the true way . . . I cannot be silent (true love and pure life stirring in me and moving me), but am necessitated to testify of it to others;

and this is it: to retire inwardly, and wait to feel somewhat of the Lord, somewhat of his holy spirit and power, discovering and drawing from that which is contrary to him, and into his holy nature and heavenly image.

The main thing in religion is to receive a principle of life from God, whereby the mind may be changed, and the heart made able to understand the mysteries of his kingdom, and to see and walk in the way of life; and this is the travail of the souls of the righteous, that they may abide, grow up, and walk with the Lord in this principle; and that others also, who breathe after him, may be gathered into, and feel the virtue of, the same principle.

But there is one that stands in the way to hinder this work of the Lord, who with great subtility strives to keep souls in captivity, and to prejudice them against the precious living appearances of the redeeming power of the Lord.

One great way whereby he doth this is, by raising up in them a fear lest they should be deceived and betrayed, and instead of obtaining more, lose that little of God which they have. With this was I exercised long; and still, when life stirred in my heart, then this fear was raised in me; so that I durst not in judgment close with what secretly in spirit I felt to be of God, it having a true touch of his quickening, warming, convincing, enlivening virtue in it.

Now, he that would meet with the true religion, the religion of the gospel, must meet with the power, receive the power, believe, dwell, and act in the power. For Christ was made a king, a priest, and prophet, not after the law of a carnal commandment, but after the power of an endless life: and his covenant is not like the old, in word or letter; but in the same power and life wherein the priests were made ministers.

So the knowledge here, the faith here, the hope here . . . are not literal, but living. He that receiveth this knowledge, receiveth living knowledge. This faith gives victory over unbelief, and over that spirit whose strength lies in unbelief. This hope purifies the heart even as he is pure. And he that receiveth the righteousness of this covenant, receiveth a living garment, which hath power in it over death and unrighteousness. The beginning of this religion, of this power and holy inward covenant, is sweet; but the pure progress and going on of it much more pleasant, as the Lord gives to feel the growth and sweet living freshness of it; notwithstanding the temptations, fears, troubles, trials, oppositions, and great dangers, both within and without, . . . all its ways are pleasantness, and its paths peace; yea, the very yoke is easy and the burden light, when the mind and will is changed by the power, and helped and assisted by the Lord in its subjection to the power.

The Lord is now gentle and tender, pursuing thee with his love, and following thee up and down with his light. And though thou run from him into sin and transgression, and hearken to the wisdom of the flesh, yet his voice comes after thee to reclaim thee; and if thou wilt hear, and but yield thyself to him, he will not put thee to do any thing, but subdue all thy enemies for thee; yea, he will slay the serpentine wisdom in thee, with all its inventions, and dash all the children of Babylon against the stones, without pity to them, though with great pity to thee.

Therefore take heed of the fleshly wisdom; take heed of thine own understanding; take heed of thy reasoning or disputing; for these are the weapons wherewith the witness is slain. That wisdom must be destroyed, and that understanding brought to naught, and thou become a child, and learn as a child if ever thou know the things of God.

Yea, there are some who are grievously sick in soul, and deeply wounded in spirit, the sadness and misery of whose condition cries aloud for the help of the physician. Now the eye and heart of the Lord is more especially towards these; and so he bids his prophets be instructing and comforting these, concerning the salvation, the healing, the oil of gladness, the Messiah to come; and when he comes, he sends him up and down to seek out these, to keep company with these, to help and relieve these; having given him the tongue of the learned, to speak a word in season to these weary distressed ones. These are not like the common, rough, unhewn, knotty, rugged earth; but like earth prepared for the seed, and so easily and naturally receive it. The gospel is preached to others at a distance; which, it is true, they may have, if they will hearken to it, and wait for it, and part with what must first be parted with; but they have a great way to travel thither. But these are near the kingdom; these are near that which opens, and lets in life; these are quickly reached to, melted, and brought into the sense in which with joy they receive the faith, and with the faith the power which brings righteousness and salvation to their souls.

116

2

FAITH

THERE is a faith which is of a man's self, and a faith which is the gift of God; or, a power of believing which is found in the nature of fallen man, and a power of believing which is given from above. As there are two births, the first and the second, so they have each their faith, . . . and seem to lay hold on the same thing for life; and the contention about the inheritance will not be ended, till God determine it.

Therefore observe and consider well, what this faith which is of a man's self can do; and how far it may go in the changing of man, and in producing a conformity of him to the letter of the Scriptures. And then consider where it is shut out, what it cannot do, what change it cannot make, and what it cannot conform to, that so the true distinction may be let into the mind, and not a foundation laid of so great a mistake in a matter of so great concernment.

A man may believe the history of the Scriptures, yea, and all the doctrines of them (so far as he can reach them with his understanding) with this faith which is of man . . . As by this faith a man can receive doctrines of instruction out of philosophers' books, so by the same faith he may receive doctrines of instructions out of the Scriptures. . . .

This being believed from the relation of the history

of these things, it naturally sets all the powers of man on work . . . towards the avoiding of misery and the attaining of happiness. . . . Must he pray? He will pray. Must he hear? He will hear. Must he read? He will read. Must he meditate? He will meditate. Must he deny himself and all his own righteousness and duties, and hope only for salvation in the merits of Christ? He will seem to do that too, and say, when he has done all he can, he is but an unprofitable servant. Does the Scripture say he can do nothing without the Spirit? He will acknowledge that too, and he hopes he has the Spirit. . . . Thus man by a natural faith grows up and spreads into a great tree, and is very confident and much pleased, not perceiving the defect in his root, and what all his growth here will come to.

This being done with much seriousness and industry, there must needs follow a great change in man; his understanding will be more and more enlightened, his will more and more conformed to that to which he thus gives himself up. . . . He will find a kind of life and growth in this according to its kind. . . .

Now how easy is it for a man to mistake here, and call this the truth. . . . He sees a change made by this in him, and this he accounts the true conversion and regeneration. . . . Though it may seem to have unity with all the Scriptures in the letter, yet it cannot have unity with one Scripture in the life. . . . So it may have a literal knowledge of the blood of Christ, and of justification; but the life of the blood which livingly justifieth, that birth cannot feel, but can only talk of it, according to the relation it reads in the Scriptures. . . . And here is the great contention in the world between these two births: the one contending for their knowledge in the letter, and the other contending for their knowledge in the life; the one setting up their faith from the natural part, calling it spiritual; and the other, who have felt the stroke of God upon this (and thereby come to know the difference), setting up the faith of the true heir.

In plain terms, you must part with all your religion which you have gathered in your own wisdom . . . and which only can make a fair show in the dark but cannot endure the searching light of the day of the Lord, and ye must purchase the true religion, the true righteousness, the true innocency and purity of Christ. The old must be done away, truly done away, and the new come in the place, so that flesh and self may be quite destroyed, and nothing but Christ found in you, and you found nowhere but in Christ, if you enter his kingdom; for no unclean thing can enter. Therefore, put away pride and passion and enmity and fleshly reasonings, and seek out that which is pure, and enter into it, and take up the cross against all that is contrary, that so you may be wrought into it, and found in it . . . and come to that which is infallible. And know the silencing of the fleshly part, that the spiritual part may grow in the wisdom, that so ye may learn in the spirit, and know the word of God, and be able to speak it.

Truth is of God, and was with God, and in God, before anything else had a being. Truth was before error or deceit; for it was from the truth that the error was, and it was about truth that the deceit was. There was somewhat which erred from truth, and brought deceit into the world, and hath propagated deceit in the world; but truth remains the same that it was, keeping its pure, eternal, unchangeable nature, and is not, nor ever was, nor ever can be defiled or tainted with any error or deceit, but testifieth against it, reproveth it;

and condemneth for it, draweth out of it, and delivereth from its bonds and captivity all those that hearken and cleave to it, in the faith which is of its nature and begetting.

Now, is not this a pearl? Nay, is not this the pearl indeed, the precious pearl of price? Who would not buy it? Who would not sell all for it? Who would not dig in the field where this treasure is hid, until he find it? The field is near thee, O man, which thou art to purchase and dig in, and must feel torn up by the plough of God in some measure before this pearl or treasure appear to thee; and thou must take up and bear the yoke and cross of Christ, until all be bowed down and crucified in thee which is contrary to its nature, before it be polished in thee, and thou come to behold and enjoy its riches and everlasting fulness. Oh, happy are they that are begotten and born of it! happy are they that know its voice, and give up to it, to be gathered and redeemed by it, out of all deceits, out of all errors, out of all that entangles and ensnares the soul in sin, misery, and utter perdition; for destruction and misery everlasting is out of it, and life and salvation is alone to be found in it.

Now to the soul that hath felt breathings towards the Lord formerly, and in whom there are yet any true breathings left after his living presence, and after the feeling of his eternal virtue in the heart, I have this to say: "Where art thou? Art thou in thy soul's rest? Dost thou feel the virtue and power of the gospel? Dost thou feel the ease which comes from the living arm, to the heart which is joined to it in the light of the gospel? Is thy laboring for life in a good degree at an end? And dost thou feel the life and power flowing in upon thee from the free fountain? Is the load really taken off from thy back? Dost thou find the captive redeemed and set free from the power of sin, and the captivity broken, and he which led thee captive from the life and from the eternal power now led captive by the life and by the redeeming power, which is eternal? Hast thou found this, or hast thou missed of it? Let thine heart answer." Ah! do not imagine and talk away the rest and salvation of thy soul. The gospel state is a state of substance, a state of enjoying the life, a state of feeling the presence and power of the Lord in his pure holy spirit, a state of binding up, a state of healing, a state of knowing the Lord and walking with him in the light of his own spirit. It begins in a sweet, powerful touch of life, and there is a growth in the life (in the power, in the divine virtue, in the rest, peace, and satisfaction of the soul in God) to be administered and waited for daily. Now art thou here, in the living power, in the divine life, joined to the spring of life, drawing water of life out of the well of life with joy? Or art thou dry, dead, barren, sapless, or at best but unsatisfiedly mourning after what thou wantest?

3

THE SEED

THE seed of God is the word of God; the seed of the kingdom is the word of the kingdom. It is a measure of the light and life, of the grace and truth, which is by Jesus Christ, whereof in him is the fulness. It is a heavenly talent, or manifestation of his spirit in the heart, which is given to man for him, in the virtue and strength of Christ, to improve for God. This which God hath placed in man, to witness for himself, and to guide man from evil unto good (in the pure breathings, quickenings, and shinings of it), this is the seed, which is freely bestowed on man, to spring up and remain in him, and to gather him out of himself, into itself.

The pure, living, heavenly knowledge of the Father, and of his Son Christ Jesus, is wrapped up in this seed. God is light; and this seed, which comes from him, is not darkness, but light; and in the springing light of this seed, God and Christ are revealed. The divine nature of them springs up in the seed; . . . yea, here we . . . know the righteous spirit of Christ, the righteous nature of Christ, the righteous life of Christ, and feel him to be one with the Father, who begets of the same spirit, nature, and life in us. And he that is born of the spirit is spirit, and he that is united to the Lord is one spirit; and he that is united to the seed, to the measure of grace and truth from Christ (wherein and whereby the soul is united), is united to God, and ingrafted into Christ; and as the seed is formed in him, Christ is formed in him; and as he is formed and new-created in the seed, he is the workmanship of God, formed and new-created in Christ.

What is the nature of the seed of God, or the seed of the kingdom?

Though the nature of it hath been largely signified already, under the foregoing head, . . . yet I shall speak a little more punctually and expressly of it in several particulars, according to the Scriptures, that the reader may have the more distinct sense and inward apprehension of it, the Lord opening his heart in reading these things.

1. It is of an immortal, incorruptible nature (I Peter i. 23). It is a seed that can never die in itself, though it may be as it were dead in man, or unto man, not putting forth any of its hidden life or virtue in the man that hath slain it as to himself; who, having slain that whereby God gives life, is dead in trespasses and in sins, and cannot live any more, till God breathe upon and quicken this seed in him, and him by this seed. This is a great mystery. Doubtless the seed of life and godliness, wherein the life and godliness of the soul lies hid, must needs be a great mystery, and cannot be known but as God reveals it.

2. It's of a gathering nature. It is of the nature of a net (Matt. xiii. 47). It gathers out of that which is contrary to God, unto God. It gathers out of the world, out of the sea of wickedness, out of the kingdom of darkness, out of a man's own nature and spirit, into God's nature and spirit, and his light and kingdom, wherein the soul should dwell, and walk, and be subject, with God.

3. It is of a purging, cleansing nature. It is of the nature of fire, of the nature of water, inwardly and spiritually. This seed is spirit and life in a measure; and by it, or by God's spirit which dwells and is revealed in it, he washeth and purgeth away the filth of the daughter of Sion, and the blood of Jerusalem from the midst thereof. There is strength in this seed, and virtue in this seed, against all the strength of deceit and wickedness in the other seed; and as it springs up, and is received and joined to in the holy fear of the Lord, it prevails over it, and casteth away its darkness, and purgeth away and burneth up its filth, chaff, and corruption.

4. It is of a seasoning, leavening, sanctifying nature. It is like salt, it is like leaven. It seasons and leavens with life. It seasons and leavens with righteousness. It seasons and leavens with the image of God. So soon as ever it springs in the heart, it begins to leaven it; and if it be not snibbed, or grieved, or hurt, or quenched (for it is of a most sensible, tender nature), it will go on leavening more and more with the nature of truth, into the likeness of the God of truth (Mark ix. 50; Luke xiii. 21; Col. iv. 6).

5. It is of an enriching nature. It is a hidden treasure or pearl of great price. It makes the wise merchant very rich, who sells all for it, and buys the field and it. He that buys the truth, and will by no means sell or part with it, but gives up to it, and makes it his treasure, oh, how doth it enrich his heart with that which is holy and heavenly! How rich doth it make him towards God (Matt. xiii. 44-46)!

6. It is of an improving, growing nature, of a nature that will grow and may be improved. The one talent may be increased into more. The little seed, like a grain of mustard seed, will grow in the good ground beyond

124

all herbs and become a tree, a tree of righteousness of the Lord's planting, that he may be glorified (Matt. xiii. 31, 32; xxv. 16; viii. 23).

But what need I mention any more? Here is light, here is life, here is righteousness, here is peace, here is heavenly joy, here is the holy power, springing and bringing forth their fruits and precious operations and effects in the heart; and here is assurance of the love of God in Christ forever, and that God will never leave nor forsake that soul which is joined to him, and abides with him in this seed; but it shall be kept by the power of God, through the faith that springs from this seed, unto perfect redemption and salvation. *Amen.*

4

DOCTRINES

NOW, friends, this is an excellent thing indeed to come to and be acquainted with, and receive, that which the Scriptures testify of, to wit, to receive Christ, to feel union with him in his spirit, to enter into the new and holy agreement with God, into the everlasting covenant of life and peace, to feel the partition wall broken down, and the wall of salvation reared up, and the defense which is thereby; to find the law of God, the law of life, the law of the new creation, written in the heart; the pure fear planted there by God, which keepeth the mind and spirit from departing from him; to have his spirit put within, causing to walk in his ways, and to keep his statutes and judgments, and do them; and so to have union and fellowship with the Lord.

For mark the difference between the state of the law and gospel. The law was a shadow of good things to come. The gospel is a state of enjoyment of the good things shadowed out under the law. The law was a type of the kingdom, of the spiritual kingdom of Christ, which is set up under the gospel. In John's day the kingdom was at hand; but in the day of Christ's power the kingdom is come. Under the law there was a tabernacle pitched by man; but under the gospel the true tabernacle and temple is witnessed, which God pitcheth and not man; and the holy, spiritual, heavenly sacrifices, and the living covenant, whereof Christ is the mediator, and the law written in the heart, and the spirit of the Lord put within, so that his presence is as really witnessed inwardly, in that which is truly his tabernacle and temple now, as ever it was witnessed outwardly, in his outward tabernacle and temple under the law.

Thus God did advance the state of a believer above the state of the Jews under the law; for they had the law, though written with the finger of God, yet but in tables of stone; but these have the law, written by the finger of God, in the tables of their hearts. Theirs was a law without, at a distance from them, and the priests' lips were to preserve the knowledge of it and to instruct them in it; but here is a law within, nigh at hand, the immediate light of the spirit of life shining so immediately in the heart that they need no man to teach them, but have the spirit of prophecy in themselves and quick living teachings from him continually, and are made such kings and priests to God as the state of the law did but represent. A Christian is he that comes into this substance of all the shadows contained in the law. A Christian is he that comes into this substance and lives in this substance, and in whom this substance lives. Christ is the substance who lives in the Christian, and he in Christ.

The substance, when it is shadowed out, or when it is nakedly dispensed, is one and the same thing; so that whenever it comes, it cannot be another thing than what the shadow represented it to be. Moses's dispensations and Christ's are one in spirit; and when he cometh in spirit, he doth not destroy either Moses or the prophets, but comprehends them; so that the law is but one, although the dispensations of it have been various.

What was it that was the thing of great value with the Father, in Christ giving up himself to death? It was his obedience. He did obey his Father in all things, not doing his own will, but the will of him that sent him. He was obedient to death, even the death of the cross. And so, as by one man's disobedience, death came upon all; so by the obedience of one, the free gift came upon all, which free gift is unto life; for life comes upon all that come to him, and believe in him, through the free gift, which is freely tendered to, and come upon all (Rom. v. 18, 19).

Now the Scriptures do expressly distinguish between Christ and the garment which he wore; between him that came, and the body in which he came; between the substance which was veiled, and the veil which veiled it. Lo, I come! A body hast thou prepared me. There is plainly he, and the body in which he came. There was the outward vessel, and the inward life. This we certainly know, and can never call the bodily garment Christ, but that which appeared and dwelt in the body. Now if ye indeed know the Christ of God, tell us plainly what that is which appeared in the body? Whether that was not the Christ before it took up the body, after it took up the body, and forever?

As touching free will, we know, from God, that man in his fallen estate is spiritually dead, and hath no free will to good; but his understanding and will are both darkened and captivated by the enemy. But in Christ there is freedom, and in his word there is power and life, and that reaching to the heart, looseneth the bands of the enemy, and begetteth not only a freedom of mind towards good, but an inclination, desires, and breathings after it. Thus the Father draws; and thus the soul (feeling the drawing) answers in some measure; and the soul, thus coming, is welcomed by Christ, and accepted of the Father.

There is predestination, election, calling, justifying, glorifying: predestination unto holiness, election in that which is holy, calling out of darkness into light, justifying and glorifying in the light, through the renewing and sanctification of the Spirit. All these God ordereth and manageth according to his good will, and according as he hath purposed in himself; although he be not the decreer, nor author of sin or rebellion against himself, which is the cause of the creature's condemnation.

Christ is a perfect physician, and is able to work a perfect cure on the heart that believeth in him, and waiteth upon him. Yea, he came to destroy the works of the devil, to cleanse man's mind of the darkness and power of Satan, and to fill it with the life and power of truth; and he sent forth a ministry not only for the beginning, but for the perfecting of the work: yea, his word in the mouth and heart is powerful, sharper than a two-edged sword, and he can cast out the strong man, and cut down all that is corrupt and contrary to himself, and break down every stronghold in the mind, and spoil all the goods of the enemy. Christ likewise bids his disciples be perfect, as their heavenly Father is perfect; and the apostle bids men perfect holiness in the fear of God, that they might be fully separated from, and not so much as touch, the unclean thing; but enjoy the promises of God's dwelling in them, and walking in them, whose temple under the gospel is to be pure.

In the state of perfection, the blood is not laid aside

as useless, but remains to keep pure for ever. It is the blood of the everlasting covenant. . . . Both the covenant and the blood last for ever, and are useful even to them that are perfect. And there is need and use of the faith in the blood, to believe the preservation. As the covenant itself lasts, so that which lets into and keeps in the covenant lasts also. That which unites and ties the soul to Christ the life, abides in the soul for ever, even as the union itself abides. And there is a growing in the life, even where the heart is purified from sin, even as Christ did grow and wax strong in spirit; for a state of perfection doth not exclude degrees. And so there is also a need of watching against temptations in a perfect state; for Adam was perfect, and yet he needed a watch: and Christ was perfectly pure and without sin and yet He did both watch and pray.

5

THE YOKE

THAT Christ's immediate revelation of the nature of his Father is to his babes, not to the wise, not to the zealous, not to the studious, not to the devout, not to the rich in the knowledge of the Scriptures without, but to the weak, the foolish, the poor, the lowly in heart. And man receives not these revelations by study, by reading, by willing, by running, but by being formed in the will of life, by being begotten of the will of the Father, and by coming forth in the will, and lying still in the will, and growing up in the will. Here the child receives the wisdom which is from above, and daily learns that cross which crucifies the other wisdom, which joins with and pleases the other will, which loves to be feeding on the shadowy and husky part of knowledge, without life.

Strait is the gate, narrow is the way, that leadeth unto life, and few there be that find it. The way of unbelief is broad, yea, the way of belief is broad also. It is easy for a man so to believe concerning Christ, or in Christ (as his heart may call it), as to miss of the nature of the true faith, and of the sweet and blessed effects which accompany it. It is easy likewise to miss the yoke (to take up a wrong yoke, in the self-will, self-wisdom, self-interpretation of Scriptures), or easy starting aside from the true yoke; but it is hard coming under the yoke of the life, and hard abiding under it. Again, it is easy mis-learning: a man may so read, and so hear, as that he may be always learning, and never come to the knowledge of the truth; never come to the truth as it is received and held in Jesus, but may so get and hold the knowledge of the truth, as man in his wisdom may get and hold it from the letter. And if a man thus miss the way, how can he attain the end? If a man begin not in the true faith, in the living faith, how can he attain the rest which the true faith alone leads to? If a man miss of the yoke, or abide not constantly under the yoke, how can he meet with the true ease and rest which is in it, and which it alone can administer? If a man learn not the truth aright of the true teacher, how can he ever reap the effects of the true knowledge?

Christ hath plainly chalked out the path of his rest to every weary, panting soul, which he that walketh in cannot miss of. He hath cast up, cast up; he hath made the way plain in the gospel, so plain that the wayfaring man, though a fool, yet keeping to the light of the gospel, cannot err therein, or miss of the blessed rest thereof. How is it? Why, come unto me; take my yoke upon you, and learn of me. He that walketh in this path cannot miss of it: the rest is at the end of it, nay, the rest is in it: he that believeth entereth into the rest. The true faith, the faith which stands in the power, and which is given to the birth which is born from above, is the substance of the rest hoped for, and there is a true taste and some enjoyment of it given to him that truly believeth.

What is love? What shall I say of it, or how shall I in words express its nature? It is the sweetness of life;

it is the sweet, tender, melting nature of God, flowing up through his seed of life into the creature, and of all things making the creature most like unto himself, both in nature and operation. It fulfills the law, it fulfills the gospel; it wraps up all in one, and brings forth all in the oneness. It excludes all evil out of the heart, it perfects all good in the heart. A touch of love doth this in measure; perfect love doth this in fulness. But how can I proceed to speak of it? Oh, that the souls of all that fear and wait on the Lord might feel its nature fully, and then would they not fail of its sweet, over-coming operations, both towards one another, and to-wards enemies. The great healing, the great conquest, the great salvation is reserved for the full manifestation of the love of God. His judgments, his cuttings, his hewings by the word of his mouth are but to prepare for, but not to do, the great work of raising up the sweet building of his life, which is to be done in love, and in peace, and by the power thereof. And this my soul waits and cries after, even the full springing up of eternal love in my heart, and in the swallowing of me wholly into it, and the bringing of my soul wholly forth in it, that the life of God in its own perfect sweetness may freely run forth through this vessel, and not be at all tinctured by the vessel, but perfectly tincture and change the vessel into its own nature; and then shall no fault be found in my soul before the Lord, but the spotless life be fully enjoyed by me, and become a perfectly pleasant sacrifice to my God.

Oh, how sweet is love! How pleasant is its nature! How takingly doth it behave itself in every condition, upon every occasion, to every person, and about every-thing! How tenderly, how readily, doth it help and serve the meanest! How patiently, how meekly, doth it

133

bear all things, either from God or man, how unexpectedly soever they come, or how hard soever they seem! How doth it believe, how doth it hope, how doth it excuse, how doth it cover even that which seemeth not to be excusable, and not fit to be covered! How kind is it even in its interpretations and charges concerning miscarriages! It never over-chargeth, it never grates upon the spirit of him whom it reprehends; it never hardens, it never provokes; but carrieth a meltingness and power of conviction with it. This is the nature of God; this, in the vessels capacitated to receive and bring it forth in its glory, the power of enmity is not able to stand against, but falls before, and is overcome by.

That poverty and humility of spirit, which springeth from the same root from which the faith, the love, the peace, the joy, and the other heavenly things arise, and is of the same nature. There is a voluntary humility, and a voluntary poverty, even of spirit, which man casts himself into, and forms in himself, by his own workings and reasonings. This is not the true, but the false image, or counterfeit of the true; but then there is a poverty which ariseth from God's emptying the creature, from God's stripping the creature; and a humility which ariseth from a new heart and nature. This is of the right kind, and is lasting, and abides in the midst of the riches and glory of the kingdom. For as Christ was poor in spirit before his Father, and lowly in heart in the midst of all the fulness which he received from him; so it is with those who are of the same birth and nature with Christ. They are filled with humility and clothed with humility, in the midst of all the graces and heavenly riches which God fills them and adorns them with. Keep in the faith, keep in the truth, keep in the light, keep in the power. It excludes boasting in or after the flesh, and keeps the mind in that humility and poverty of spirit which God hath brought, and daily further and further brings, it into. And so the humility and poverty remains (poor in spirit for ever, humble in spirit for ever, nothing before the Lord for ever), even as that remains which brought into that frame, and keeps in that frame forever. And so the Lord of Life is only exalted, and the creature kept abased before him, and low forever; and is nothing but as the Lord pleaseth to fill, and make it to be what it is.

6

WORSHIP

AND this is the manner of their worship. They are to wait upon the Lord, to meet in the silence of flesh, and to watch for the stirrings of his life, and the breakings forth of his power amongst them. And in the breakings forth of that power they may pray, speak, exhort, rebuke, sing, or mourn, and so on, according as the spirit teaches, requires, and gives utterance. But if the spirit do not require to speak, and give to utter, then everyone is to sit still in his place (in his heavenly place I mean) feeling his own measure, feeding thereupon, receiving therefrom (into his spirit) what the Lord giveth. Now in this is edifying, pure edifying, precious edifying; his soul who thus waits is hereby particularly edified by the spirit of the Lord at every meeting. And then also there is the life of the whole felt in every vessel that is turned to its measure; insomuch as the warmth of life in each vessel doth not only warm the particular, but they are like an heap of fresh and living coals, warming one another, insomuch as a great strength, freshness, and vigor of life flows into all. And if any be burthened, tempted, buffeted by Satan, bowed down, overborne, languishing, afflicted, distressed, and so on, the estate of such is felt in spirit, and secret cries or open (as the Lord pleaseth), ascend up to the Lord for them, and they many times find ease and relief, in a few words spoken, or without words, if it be the season of their help and relief with the Lord.

For absolutely silent meetings (wherein there is a resolution not to speak) we know not; but we wait on the Lord, either to feel him in words, or in silence of spirit without words, as he pleaseth. And that which we aim at, and are instructed to by the spirit of the Lord as to silent meetings, is that the flesh in everyone be kept silent, and that there be no building up, but in the spirit and power of the Lord.

Our worship is a deep exercise of our spirits before the Lord, which doth not consist in an exercising the natural part or natural mind, either to hear or speak words, or in praying according to what we, of ourselves, can apprehend or comprehend concerning our needs; but we wait, in silence of the fleshly part, to hear with the new ear what God shall please to speak inwardly in our own hearts, or outwardly through others, who speak with the new tongue which he unlooseth and teacheth to speak; and we pray in the spirit, and with the new understanding, as God pleaseth to quicken, draw forth, and open our hearts towards himself.

Thus our minds being gathered into the measure, or gift of grace, which is by Jesus Christ; here we appear before our God, and here our God, and his Christ, is witnessed in the midst of us.

This is that gathering in the name, which the promise is to, where we meet together, waiting with one consent on the Father of Life, bowing and confessing to him in the name of his Son; and that fleshly part, that fleshly understanding, that fleshly wisdom, that fleshly will, which will not bow, is chained down, and kept under by the power of life which God stretcheth forth over it, and subdueth it by. So then, there is the sweet communion enjoyed, the sweet love flowing, the sweet peace of spirit reaped, which the Father breathes upon, and gives to his children; the sweet joy and refreshment in the Lord our righteousness, who causeth righteousness to drop down from heaven, and truth to spring up out of the earth. And so our Father is felt blessing us, blessing our land, blessing our habitations, delighting in us and over us to do us good; and our land yields its increase to the Lord of Life, who hath redeemed it and planted the precious plants and seeds of life in it.

Give over thine own willing, give over thine own running, give over thine own desiring to know or be anything, and sink down to the seed which God sows in thy heart and let that be in thee, and grow in thee, and breathe in thee, and act in thee, and thou shalt find by sweet experience that the Lord knows that and loves and owns that, and will lead it to the inheritance of life, which is his portion.

Lord, take care of all thy children. Oh, thou tender Father, consider what they suffer for the testimony of thy truth, and for thy name's sake, and uphold them, and give them victory, and a holy dominion over all, because it belongs to thy seed into which thou hast gathered them, and in which thou hast united them to thyself. Oh, carry on thy glorious work, which thy own mighty arm hath begun, and cut it short in righteousness for thine Elect's sake, that it may be finished by thee, to thine own everlasting praise. Thy children wait on thee, they cry to thee day and night, that they may be preserved by thee in the well-doing, and in the pure, holy, innocent sufferings for thy truth's sake; until thou say, "It is enough," until thy Holy Spirit say, "It is finished, my lambs, ye shall suffer no more, but now ye shall reign with me and my Son for ever."

Christ is the minister of the true sanctuary, which God hath pitched, and not man. There is a city whose builder and maker is God. The foundation stone, the cornerstone, the top stone of this city or building is Christ. He, therefore, that would know Christ, and be built upon Christ, must find a holy thing revealed in his heart, and his soul built thereon by him who alone can raise this building, who can rear up the tabernacle that hath long been fallen down, who can build up the old waste places, and restore the paths for the ransomed and redeemed of the Lord to walk and travel on in.

Therefore the great work of the minister of Christ is to keep the conscience open to Christ, and to preserve men from receiving any truths of Christ as from them further than the spirit opens, or to imitate any of their practices further than the spirit leads, guides, and persuades them. For persons are exceeding prone to receive things as truths from those whom they have a high opinion of, and to imitate their practices, and so hurt their own growth and endanger their souls. For if I receive a truth before the Lord, by his spirit, make it manifest to me, I lose my guide and follow but the counsel of the flesh, which is exceeding greedy of receiving truths and running into religious practices without the spirit. Therefore the main thing in religion is to keep the conscience pure to the Lord, to know the guide, to follow the guide, to receive from him the light whereby I am to walk; and not to take things for truths because others see them to be truths, but to wait till the spirit make them manifest to me; nor to run into worships, duties, performances, or practices, because others are led thither, but to wait till the spirit lead me thither. He that makes haste to be rich (even in religion, running into knowledge, and into worships and performances, before he feel a true and clear guidance) shall not be innocent; nor the Lord will not hold him guiltless, when he comes to visit, for spiritual adultery and idolatry.

He that keeps not a day, may unite in the same spirit, in the same life, in the same love with him that keeps a day; and he who keeps a day, may unite in heart and soul with the same spirit and life in him who keeps not a day; but he that judgeth the other because of either of these, errs from the spirit, from the love, from the life, and so breaks the bond of unity. And he that draws another to any practice before the life in his own particular lead him doth, as much as in him lies, destroy the soul of that person.

Let nothing judge in thee (concerning thine own heart, or concerning others, or concerning any way or truth of God) but only the begotten of God in the heart. Let the light in which thou art begotten to God, and which shines upon his begotten, be the only judge in thee, and then thou canst not err in judgment. Be not hasty, be not forward in judgment, keep back to the life, still waiting for the appearance and openings of the life. A few steps fetched in the life and power of God are much safer and sweeter than a hasty progress in the hasty forward spirit.

True obedience, gospel obedience, flows from life, flows from the living faith. If I could obey in all things that God requires of me, yet that would not satisfy me, unless I felt my obedience flow from the birth of His life in me. "My Father doth all in me," saith Christ.

This was Christ's comfort. And to feel Christ do all in the soul is the comfort of everyone that truly believes in him.

Canst thou pray? How camest thou to learn to pray? Wast thou taught from above? Or didst thou gain the skill and ability by the exercise and improvement of thine own natural part? Didst thou begin with sighs and groans, staying there till the same spirit that taught thee to groan, taught thee also to speak? Wast thou ever able to distinguish the sighs and groans of the spirit's begetting from the sighs and groans of thy own natural and affectionate part?

Prayer is the breath of the living child to the Father of Life, in that spirit which quickened it, which giveth it the right sense of its wants, and suitable cries proportionable to its state, in the proper season thereof. So that mark: Prayer is wholly out of the will of the creature; wholly out of the time of the creature; wholly out of the power of the creature; in the spirit of the Father, who is the fountain of life, and giveth forth breathings of life to his child at his pleasure.

7

TESTIMONIES

THE works that flow from God's good spirit, the works that are wrought in God, they are good works; the works of the new birth, of the new creature, are good works; whereas all the works of the flesh are bad, though never so finely painted. All its thoughts, imaginations, reasonings, willings, runnings, hunting to find out God and heavenly things, with all its sacrifices, are corrupt and evil, having of the bad leaven, of the bad nature in them. Make the tree good, or its fruit can never be good; so that they are only the good works that flow from the good tree, from the good root.

There is a continual praying unto God. There is a continual blessing and praising of his name, in eating, or drinking, or whatever else is done. There is a continual bowing to the majesty of the Lord in every thought, in every word, in every action, though it be in worldly things and occasions; yet the spirit of the Lord is seen there, and the tongue confesseth him there, and the knee boweth to him there. This is the true worship, and this is the rest or Sabbath wherein the true worshippers worship.

The church is called into the liberty of the gospel, and her children are born of the word immortal, and of the truth which makes free; and it is not the church's nature either to receive or impose yokes of bondage, but to stand fast, and to exhort all her members to stand fast, in the liberty wherewith Christ hath made them free. But where there is any thing unruly, or contrary to the power, that is to be yoked down by the power.

And the particular waiting upon God in his Holy Spirit, light, and power, the spirit, light, and power, will discover what is disorderly, and unruly, and not of God in the particular, and lay a yoke upon it. The church also waiting upon God, in their meetings together in his name, the Lord will discover what is hurtful to the body, and contrary to the life of the body, and lay yokes upon it; and he that refuseth this yoke, keeps alive that which is impure and fleshly, and keeps down the just in himself.

There are some considerations springing up in my heart concerning unity . . . which are as follows:

Unity in the spiritual body, which is gathered into and knit together in the pure life, is a most natural and comely thing. Yea, it is exceeding lovely to find all that are of the Lord of one heart, of one mind, of one judgment, in one way of practice and order in all things.

The Lord is to be waited upon for the bringing forth of this in the body; that as there is a foundation of it laid in all (the life and spring being over all), so all may be brought by him into the true and full oneness.

The Lord is to be acknowledged and praised in the bringing of it forth (so far as it is brought forth), and to be waited upon for the further perfecting of it.

A watch is to be kept (throughout the whole body, and in every heart) for the preserving of it, so far as it is brought forth, that the enemy, by no device or subtility, cause disunion or difference in any respect, wherein there was once a true unity and oneness. For the enemy will watch to divide; and if he be not watched against, in that which is able to discover and keep him out, by some device or other he will take his advantage to make a rent (in those that are not watchful) from the pure truth and unity of life in the body. For he that in the least thing rents from the body (in any respect or particular which was brought forth by the life), he in that respect hearkens to another spirit (even the dividing spirit) and by its instigation rents from the life itself, and so doth not keep his habitation, nor his unity, with that which abides in its habitation.

He which is born of God, he who is of the love, and in the love, cannot but be tender. He who is born of the earthly wisdom, who taketh up and holdeth forth a religion there, cannot but persecute. Why so? Because he cannot but judge that any man may take up religion as he hath done, and so, by reasonings, may come to acknowledge and take up what he hath taken up, and holdeth forth, or else he is wilful and stubborn, as he judgeth. But now he that is born of God, and hath received his light, knowledge, religion, and way of worship from him, he knoweth that no man can rightly receive them but the same way, to wit, from God, by the light which he causeth to shine into the heart at his pleasure, and in the faith which he gives. So that God's free and powerful spirit is to be waited upon, for the working of all in his people, and not any forced to act beyond, or contrary to, the principle of his life and light in them.

Yet the government of Christ and his kingdom is not

opposite to any just government of a nation or people. Christ's government is a righteous government of the heart, or inner man, chiefly; which doth not oppose a righteous government of the outward man. Nay, those who are Christ's subjects, and singly obedient to his law of righteousness in their spirits, are more faithful to men, and more subject to any just law of government, than others can be; for their fidelity and subjection is out of love, and for conscience sake. But this is which offends the world; men many times make laws in their own will, and according to their own wisdom (now the wisdom of the world is corrupt, and hath erred from the guidance of God), and are not free from self-ends and interests, not being gathered into that which cleanseth and keepeth pure the naturals. Now that which is of God cannot bow to any thing which is corrupt in man. It can lie down and suffer, and bear the plowing of long and deep furrows upon its back; but it cannot act that which is against its life. It cannot be disloyal to its king, to gratify the spirit of this world; but what practice or testimony its king calls for against the evil and corruption of this world, it must obey singly and faithfully.

As government came from God, so the righteous execution of it depends upon God. Every man needs God's help daily, else he may easily err in his course; and governments and governors need God's help much more, in the many intricacies and perplexities which they often meet with. And God is nigh to them in their difficult cases, who wait upon him for counsel and direction. If the case be knotty, yet if God give wisdom, hath the magistrate cause to complain? And will not the Lord assist that magistrate, who in his fear waits on him, and is not willing to spare the evil, and afraid to hurt the good? If there were not so much consulting with man's wisdom and policy (nor such laying of designs and intents at first as spring from man and not from God), but a naked, upright waiting on him for instruction, who can only guide the spirit of man aright, governments would not prove so difficult, nor the success therein so dangerous.

Their way of determining things at last (which is by a vote of the major part) is an uncertain way of determination; for it is not impossible that the major part may be over-swayed by by-ends, and in relation to their own advantage and interest, against the righteousness and equity of the reason of the lesser part; so that the way of determining things by a council is not a certain way in itself: but because men know not well how to find out a better and more probable way of deciding controversies, they judge it necessary to acquiesce therein. But the votes and determinations of men concerning a thing do not conclude a thing to be true or false in itself; they only signify their opinion, judgment, and testimony concerning the thing. . . .

The dictate of conscience is not made a plea by us, but the answering and obeying the light of Christ in our consciences is that which keepeth them void of offence, both towards God and towards men. Now it is one thing for a man to act evil, and plead it is his conscience; and it is another thing for a man to be guided by the infallible light of the spirit; or, if he be not come so far, yet to be made tender in his heart towards Christ concerning his practices in religion. In this last case we say that in things whose good or evil chiefly depends upon the knowledge and persuasion of the mind, which Christ alone can do, here Christ is the sole lord and judge of the conscience (Rom. xiv, 4), and not either minister, church, or magistrate. Christ giveth knowledge, Christ increaseth knowledge, and Christ requireth obedience according to the knowledge given or increased.

Fighting is not suitable to a gospel spirit; but to the spirit of the world, and the children thereof. The fighting in the gospel is turned inward against the lusts, and not outward against the creatures. There is to be a time when nation shall not lift up sword against nation, neither shall they learn war any more. When the power of the gospel spreads over the whole earth, thus shall it be throughout the earth; and where the power of the spirit takes hold of and overcomes any heart at present, thus will it be at present with that heart. This blessed state, which shall be brought forth in the general in God's season, must begin in particulars; and they therein are not prejudicial to the world (nor would be so looked upon, if the right eye in man were but open to see with), but emblems of that blessed state which the God of glory hath promised to set up in the world in the days of the gospel.

Israel of old stood not by their strength and wisdom and preparations against their enemies, but in quietness and confidence and waiting on the Lord for direction, and shall not such now, who are true Israelites, and have indeed attained to the true gospel state, follow the Lord in the peaceable life and spirit of the gospel unless they see by rational demonstration beforehand how they shall be preserved therein? I speak not this against any magistrate's or people's defending themselves against foreign invasions, or making use of the sword to suppress the violent and evildoers within their borders (for this the present estate of things may and doth require, and a great blessing will attend the sword where it is borne uprightly to that end, and its use will be honorable; and while there is need of a sword, the Lord will not suffer that government, or those governors, to want fitting instruments under them for the managing thereof, to wait on him in his fear to have the edge of it rightly directed). But yet there is a better state, which the Lord hath already brought some into, and which nations are to expect and travel towards. Yea, it is far better to know the Lord to be the defender, and to wait on him daily, and see the need of his strength, wisdom, and preservation, than to be ever so strong and skilful in weapons of war.

This, then, is the sum of our answer in this respect: we are not against the true life and power of godliness, wherever it hath appeared, or yet appears, under the veil of any form whatsoever. Nay, all persons who singly wait upon the Lord in the simplicity and sincerity of their hearts, whether under any form, or out of forms (that matters little to us), are very dear unto us in the Lord. But we are against all forms, images, imitations, and appearances which betray the simplicity and sincerity of the heart, keep the life in bondage, and endanger the loss of the soul. And too many such now there are, which hold the immortal seed of life in captivity under death, over which we cannot but mourn, and wait for its breaking off the chains, and its rising out of all its graves into its own pure life, power, and fulness of liberty in the Lord.

8

CONCLUSION

AND so at length we came to witness (abiding the trial of this dreadful day, wherein our God appeared to us as a consuming fire) a new heaven and a new earth inwardly; and no more sea of wickedness, no more sea of inward trouble, but righteousness, peace, and joy inwardly and our God becoming a rich portion to us, watching over us in most tender care and love, and delighting in us to do us good, making known to us the riches of the gospel, even the feast of fat things; and giving us to partake of the well or fountain of living waters in our own hearts, which springs up freshly in us daily unto life eternal. So that we were not only invited to the waters, but taught also to come thereto; and when we came, we were not sent away empty, but had the water of life given us; which became such a well as out of it flow streams of living water. Ah, blessed be the Lord! Did we ever think, in our dry, dead, barren estate, to have seen such a day as this?

All people upon earth who love your souls, and have any true secret pantings after God, look to the nature of your spirits, and look to the nature of those things ye let into your minds; lest ye take death for life, error for truth, and so sow to yourselves corruption and rear up a fabric in Mystery Babylon, which will be turned into desolation and utter ruins by the power of life from Sion.

Propositions concerning the Only Way of Salvation:

That there is no way of being saved from sin, and wrath eternal, but by that Christ alone who died at Jerusalem. . . .

That there is no way of being saved by him, but through receiving him into the heart by a living faith, and having him formed in the heart. . . .

That there is no way of receiving Christ into the heart and of having him formed there, but by receiving the light of his spirit, in which light he is and dwells. . . .

That the way of receiving the light of the spirit into the heart is by hearkening to, and receiving, its convictions of sin there.

How faith, or believing in the light, worketh out the salvation:

It causeth a fear and trembling to seize upon the sinner. The Lord God Almighty, by the rising of his light in the heart, causeth the powers of darkness to shake . . . and then the plant of the Lord springs up out of the dry and barren ground. . . .

In this fear and trembling the work of true repentance and conversion is begun and carried on. There is a turning of the soul from the darkness to the light; from the dark power to the light power; from the spirit of deceit to the spirit of truth; from all false appearances and imaginations about holiness to that which the eternal light manifesteth to be truly so. And now is a time of mourning, of deep mourning, while the separation is working, while the enemy's strength is not broken and subdued, and the heart is now and then feeling itself still hankering after its old lovers.

In the belief of the light . . . there springs up a hope, a living hope. . . . It stays the soul in all the troubles, storms, and tempests it meets afterwards, which are many, yea, very many.

Faith through hope works righteousness, and teaches the true wisdom; and now the benefit of all the former trouble, anguish, and misery begins to be felt and the work goes on sweetly. . . .

In the righteousness, and in the true wisdom which is received in the light, there springs up a love, and a unity, and fellowship with God the Father of Lights, and with all who are children of the light. . . . And here is a willingness and power felt in this love to lay down the life even for the least truth of Christ's, or for the brethren.

Belief in the light works patience, meekness, gentleness, tenderness, and long-suffering. It will bear anything for God, anything for men's souls' sake. It will wait quietly and stilly for the carrying on of the work of God in its own soul, and for the manifestation of God's love and mercy to others. It will bear the contradiction and reproach of sinners, seeking their good, even while they are plotting, contriving, and hatching mischief, laying many subtile snares. . . .

It brings peace, joy, and glory. . . . And this is the true peace, and certain peace. . . . Here is joy, unspeakable joy, joy which the world cannot see or touch, nor the powers of darkness come near to interrupt . . . and this joy is full of glory, which glory increaseth daily more and more, by the daily sight and feeling of the living virtue and power in Christ the light, whereby the soul is continually transformed, and changed more and more out of the corruptible into the incorruptible. . . .

Here, in the light, I meet with certainty, assurance, satisfaction, yea, infallibility. I meet with the evidence and demonstration of God's spirit, which is infallible. I meet with God's witness, which is an infallible witness. I meet with God's spirit, which is an infallible spirit, who infallibly leads into all truth, and infallibly guides in the truth. I meet with an infallible shepherd, who hath an infallible voice, and gives to his sheep an infallible ear, wherewith they infallibly hear. He opens an infallible eye, and gives to it an infallible sight of God, and the heavenly mysteries of his kingdom. The spirit breathes infallibly, begets infallibly, leads infallibly, creates a new heart, a right spirit; which heart, which spirit, is of God's infallible nature, like him; for that which is born of the spirit is spirit.

But some may desire to know what I have at last met with. I answer, I have met with the seed. Understand that word, and thou wilt be satisfied, and enquire no further. I have met with my God; I have met with my Savior; and he hath not been present with me without his salvation; but I have felt the healings drop upon my soul from under his wings. I have met with the true knowledge, the knowledge of life, the living knowledge, the knowledge which is life; and this hath had the true virtue in it, which my soul hath rejoiced in, in the presence of the Lord. I have met with the seed's Father, and in the seed I have felt him my Father. There I have read his nature, his love, his compassions, his tenderness, which have melted, overcome, and changed my heart before him. I have met with the seed's faith, which hath done and doth that which the faith of man can never do. I have met with the true birth, with the birth which is heir of the kingdom, and inherits the kingdom.

I have met with the true spirit of prayer and supplication, wherein the Lord is prevailed with, and which draws from him whatever the condition needs; the soul always looking up to him in the will, and in the time and way, which is acceptable with him. What shall I say? I have met with the true peace, the true righteousness, the true holiness, the true rest of the soul, the everlasting habitation which the redeemed dwell in; and I know all these to be true, in him that is true, and am capable of no doubt, dispute, or reasoning in my mind about them; it abiding there, where it hath received the full assurance and satisfaction. And also I know very well and distinctly in spirit where the doubts and disputes are, and where the certainty and full assurance is, and in the tender mercy of the Lord am preserved out of the one, and in the other.